Don Mills has been raised up for
people hope and encouragement. T
and thoroughly researched. Readers are given an exciting preview of a rapturous delight. Don's beautiful examples and poems settle the long debate over pre-tribulation rapture. A timely treasure! Let the royal wedding begin.

Bob & Geri Boyd, Issues in Education

In these uncertain times we live in we need more than ever the reminder of, The Blessed Hope!!! It is nearer than we first believed! Don Mills in his book, *Precepts of the Blessed Hope* draws out these awesome awakening truths from the Word of God that are living water to our thirsty souls. Take time to meditate on these great writings and let the excitement of this great truth comfort your soul…

Joe Sabolick /Songwriter of "Come Just As You Are"

While many books have presented biblical evidence for a pre-tribulation rapture, *Precepts of the Blessed Hope* goes a step further, digging even deeper into God's Word. Author Don Mills presents many beautiful types, pictures, and foreshadows found throughout Scripture which affirm that the Church will be removed prior to the Tribulation. Chapters such as Types and The Elect offer wonderful biblical insights that will help the reader understand God's grand plan, consistent nature, and His promise to deliver believers from the wrath to come. This book will not only assure the Church with God's great and precious promises, but it will also challenge non-believers to consider the Lord's invitation to salvation while there is yet time.

Jim Tetlow, Eternal Productions

Precepts of the Blessed Hope

Precepts of the Blessed Hope

A View of the Types and the Great Light From Above

Don Mills

Tate Publishing & *Enterprises*

Published by Tate Publishing & Enterprises, LLC
127 E. Trade Center Terrace | Mustang, Oklahoma 73064 USA
1.888.361.9473 | www.tatepublishing.com

Tate Publishing is committed to excellence in the publishing industry. The company reflects the philosophy established by the founders, based on Psalm 68:11,
"The Lord gave the word and great was the company of those who published it."

Cover design by Amber Lee
Interior design by Joey Garrett

Published in the United States of America

ISBN: 978-1-60696-414-9
1. Religion / Christian Life / General
09.02.03

Dedication

This book is dedicated to our Lord and Savior, Jesus Christ

To his church with love and appreciation

May we see these great shadows

Revealed by the light

Table of Contents

Foreword

I read *Precepts of the Blessed Hope* over and over again, wondering why I hadn't seen all these beautiful types before. I was amazed and encouraged because I have always believed in the pre-tribulation rapture, but like everyone else I had only a small handful of Scriptures to refer to. Now God has opened up my eyes to see miles and miles of not only Scriptures, but all of these beautiful types that he's given to assure me and the rest of His bride how much Jesus loves us!

Thank you, Don Mills, and thank you, Lord Jesus, for giving Don these wonderful insights to share with all of us! I am so excited about my future - my hope is stronger than ever before! I encourage all of you to feed in the valley of these wonderful truths of God's Word.

Be blessed as you read *Precepts of the Blessed Hope*, by Don Mills!

Pastor Leo Giovinetti
Real Life Radio

Preface

Through the years, I have had many conversations with Christians who hold different views of the rapture of the church. I have watched how many times people proclaim almost gleefully that the church is going through the tribulation. I always thought it was unusual that some Christians actually seemed to have a martyr complex when discussing the rapture of the church. I have debated some of these people on website forums, and it is disturbing to see how many have rejected what the Bible has revealed through typology. They don't seem to care about the many types found throughout the Bible that point to and support the pre-trib view. They all of a sudden don't want to talk about (those) things. It's as if they've set their faces against it.

I was even accused of making up the types found in the Bible by a pre-wrath believer who evidently has closed the eyes to all of these beautiful types found throughout God's Word. Now, there is nothing wrong with having a different view of the rapture. But it is high time we recognize that there are people who say they are Christians, and yet some will have a mocking response to the pre-trib rapture of the church. They will mock what many other Christians hold to as the blessed hope. It makes you wonder if these people are caught up in the emerging church movement. That movement is very hostile to fundamental Christian beliefs especially if you believe in the pre-trib rapture of the church.

The pre-trib view is what many fundamental evangelical churches believe, and *this is the view that is attacked,* sometimes vehemently by people who say, "Where is the promise of his coming?" Or they will say, "I used to believe that, but I don't believe that anymore." It is beyond me to try to figure out where all these people are coming from, and it's not our place to judge them. I can tell you though I'm not so naive as to think that the enemy isn't clever enough to hide behind some of these ideas and from there throw rocks at the blessed hope. It seems that some people are unaware of the glorious light that is casting these great shadows that we see in the Bible.

It is the spirit of the age we live in to mock and rebel. Sometimes well-meaning Christians can get caught up in this without realizing what they are doing, and then they will start to attack other Christians for their belief in the blessed hope. Satan has been very clever in getting people to take sides to attack other believers. I am not attacking anyone but rather giving an answer for the hope that lies within me.

I've been on websites that are supposed to be Christian and watched when someone tries to share about the rapture of the church coming before the tribulation. Seemingly with no shadow of constraint these people are attacked for their view of the rapture. I have also been told on more than one occasion that the pre-trib view of the rapture is of the devil, and this is said by Christians. This shows me that first of all there is a lack of love and tolerance for other Christians; and when you go down that road, you're only embracing the spirit of the age, and that is dangerous. I generally have not seen examples of Christians who hold to a pre-trib rapture view attacking those who are not. On the other hand, I have seen the greater emphasis and a super-activated criticism by those who are of a pre-wrath or post-trib view, which are popular in the emerging church movement.

I have also noticed that many times the Scriptures are viewed with a replacement-theology view. I think this is why some people are embracing pre-wrath and post-trib views. I have come to understand that this is how many Christians have been misled in some of the last-days things; they have unwittingly replaced Israel with the church. This is completely unscriptural, but it helps explain why there are so many radical views of the Lord's coming even within the church. The emerging church movement disregards the literal fundamental view of Scripture. The emerging church is also very weak in scriptural support for the things they are trying to do and are very much against the fundamental principles of the blessed hope, which is the pre-trib rapture of the church.

Again, this is not to say that believers can't have another view of the rapture, but it is that hostile spirit that seems to be (*emerging*) that I'm writing about. This unbiblical and hostile view is what I sense, and it is definitely a part of their speech. It is because of that hostile and mocking spirit that I write with much affection on these topics and that it might benefit all my brothers and sisters in Christ. This is how these studies came about for this book. I do not accept what some people say about these topics as not being important; that's like saying the Bible is not worthy of study. "All Scripture is given by inspiration of God, and is profitable for doctrine, for reproof, for correction, for instruction in righteousness" (2 Timothy 3:16). "Through thy precepts I get understanding" (Psalm 119:104).

I didn't intend to give answers all the way through the book of Revelation because I was not led to tackle such a large subject. Many topics come up in these studies that cross over each other and support each other. I used primarily the King James translation (the received text) as there isn't a more accurate or beautiful translation to compare with. The Westcott-Hort Translation of the 1880s has caused many to stumble. They used *two main faulty manuscripts* (the codices Sinaiticus and Vaticanus) from the Catholic Church and a few others to override literally 5,700 manuscripts that the King James translators used and that were in harmony with each other.

These Catholic documents were rejected by the early church fathers at the start of the fourth century because they didn't line up with what was already handed down through the churches. This unfortunately is what the newer translations have been influenced by, and it has only caused derision; and (that was not the case before) Westcott-Hort decided they would make changes to the Bible. You can't have *two authorities* that contradict each other. Especially one that made thirty-six thousand changes in English version of KJV and six thousand changes to the Greek text.

There is a real stubbornness in some people who seem to think they can create some new thing. The Word of God cannot be taken with a smörgåsbord mentality where people take only what they want. People need to understand that the truth will be the truth whether you believe it or not; so stubbornness gets you nowhere, and creating your own genre with a certain group of people is foolishness.

This book was written to bless his church. It was not intended to come up with some new thing but rather a look into the precepts and shadows of what the Scriptures have already revealed to the saints throughout the ages. If I have misapplied anything here, then I ask for God's grace and forgiveness ahead of time. It is not my purpose to bring any more confusion to these topics but rather a loving look and a peek behind the curtain that is about to go up concerning his church.

I thank Jesus Christ, the giver of life, for his precious sacrifice upon the cross. My prayer for this book is that it will be a blessing to all Christians who want to know the truth. I hope this book will pull back the veil just enough to get a glimpse of the blessed hope that we have in our Lord Jesus. Before we leave these mortal shores, we press on, knowing full well we are in that portal of time where we must continue to preach the good news of the gospel and share the whole truth in the face of error all around us.

Golden types and precepts of old
with shadowy imagery are there foretold
Many are familiar to the types are they
They're in the Bible, understood by many straightaway
And somehow to others they seem com-
pletely foreign with nothing to say
as if from some long and bygone day,
but certainly not for today
Some have sadly forgotten to gaze at
these wonderful beautiful types
that reveal so much of his mercy in every single type
The types foreshadowed when no longer concealed
they're like fountains of truth, there now revealed
In the Holy Bible where it says of these
that were and are and are yet to be
The precepts of old are understood when
we view the type with Christ in the lens
The greatest prize awarded and yet to be found
When we look for gold nuggets and they're all around
It's then that the types are perceived in our sight
We see the clearer as it's lit up in light
We see over and over with all these imagery types
The great light casting these shadowy types

Types

God has blessed his Word with many stories that illuminate the many different aspects of Christ. We see all the typology and foreshadowing of the Lamb of God and the Jewish rituals of the temple. We see the festivals and what they represent and realize they only serve as a backdrop for the greater truths fulfilled in Christ throughout the New Testament. Studying the types is one of the most enlightening and enjoyable aspects of studying God's Word. Types and the precepts they reveal are found all throughout God's Word. They are there to help illuminate deep Bible truths that nonbelievers won't really understand, but then they are mainly for believers to meditate upon, to see the deeper things of God revealed. Jesus said to the disciples, "It is given unto you to know the mysteries of the kingdom of heaven, but to them it is not given" (Matthew 13:11). It's nice to know that at times even children can grasp the deep meanings of God because they listen to the Bible stories and get pictures in their minds about Enoch being caught up to heaven and Isaac going up the mountain to be sacrificed, and then Joseph and his coat of many colors; they see these wonderful pictures drawn in their imaginations.

There is more to studying the Bible than just line upon line. "For precept must be upon precept, precept upon precept; line upon line; here a little, and there a little" (Isaiah 28:10). If we explore the types throughout the Bible with this in mind, all of a sudden we can see the many Bible precepts once hidden from us. This study of the types is not meant to be an exhaustive study of all the types. It is meant to help all believers see the beautiful and lovely Bible types as they concern the bride of Christ.

"A Type is a Certain thing Standing with a Sacred impression set upon it by God to Signify Some good to come as Christ, or the

Gospel Concerns in this Life."[1] Types in the Bible are "a shadow of good things to come, and not the very image of the things" (Hebrews 10:1). Even holy days, the new moon, and the Sabbath are a foreshadowing. "Which are a shadow of things to come; but the body is of Christ" (Colossians 2:16–17, 1 Corinthians 10:6, 11). Speaking of the body of Christ, then what do these types of the Old Testament reveal about the substance of the bride of Christ? Do they reveal tribulation and death for the bride, or do they reveal a deep captivating love for his bride? If you're honest, you'll recognize right away what the answer is, especially after looking at these foreshadowing types found all throughout the Bible (Romans 15:4).

Today there are some Christians who don't understand that the church is the bride of Christ, as strange as that sounds. There are those who don't believe in the pre-trib rapture of the church, even though it is the most widely held view among Evangelicals. These people are left with no explanation for the types in the Bible that clearly reveal a pre-trib rapture for the bride of Christ. They cannot explain why the types in the Bible only add to a pre-trib view, and sadly, many don't seem to care what the Scriptures reveal. Their minds are made up, and don't confuse them with anything from the Word. They are left trying to explain away how Joseph married Asenath, a Gentile bride (before the seven years of famine) and how that story in the Bible doesn't reveal anything. They have no clue about what it may be revealing. They have no insight for what this might be showing. They have only a surface understanding. They have not taken a serious look at these wonderful images. It is true that one needs to endeavor to understand the types in the Bible, to lay hold of these truths for oneself, for Jesus said, "They are they that testify of me" (John 5:39). Surely the bride of Christ must be pictured in the Old Testament, but how is she revealed?

It is unfathomable how so many people have neglected to look at these picture types in the Old Testament. Do they have another explanation, or do they just ignore these stories? We cannot just shut our eyes to all the beautiful types and precepts that are presented to us throughout God's Word. We are not called to be willfully ignorant to all these precepts. As the days grow more wicked around us, let us not be content to be surface-deep Christians. We don't want to be people who have no eyes to see any of this beauty, or people that seemingly have no understanding from the types and precepts of the Old Testament.

When we look at the life of Joseph, a type of Christ in the Old Testament, we see too many comparisons in his life; even the timing of his marriage is too significant to ignore. The life of Isaac and his marriage to Rebekah is another lovely and revealing type that only shows a pre-trib position, not tribulation for his bride. Then the story of Ruth and how she so pictures the church, as a Gentile who comes to the God of Israel. She is redeemed by her kinsmen redeemer, Boaz, just as the church is redeemed by Christ. There is a comeliness within the story of Ruth, and it illuminates a true and lovely picture of the church.

"As for the Excellency of the Type: and here I say put all the types together and gather up their Excellency: and all this Excellency is but a Shadow of the Excellency of Christ. Now the things that God hath Chose have Something in General: and something more Special"[2] These types in the Bible have been recognized throughout church history by his saints. They help explain the deep intentions of God. It's as though you are fondly gazing at the photo album of God foreseeing these divine appointments. We do a grave injustice to ourselves if we disregard the clear light that shines throughout the Bible through the many types that are put in place by the Holy Spirit. Let us take seriously the intentions of God that shine through his Word when looking at the types. This chapter focuses mainly on Christ's bride and those who were Christlike in the Old Testament.

Much of the following in this chapter is from Clarence Larkin's Dispensational Truth. Reworded unless directly quoted and shown as such.

- Abraham a type of the Father
- Isaac seen as a type of Christ, "thine only son Isaac"
- Eliezer is seen as a type of the Holy Spirit sent by the Father
- Rebekah is a type of the church

- Ruth: a type of Gentile bride redeemed by kinsman redeemer
- Joseph: another picture and type of Christ
- Joseph was a shepherd as Christ is the Good Shepherd (Genesis 37:2, John 10:11).
- Both Joseph and Christ were thirty years of age when they began their ministries (Genesis 41:46, Luke 3:23).
- Joseph was "beloved" of his father (Genesis 37:3). Jesus, the beloved Son (Mark 1:11, Matthew 3:17).
- Joseph was sent to his brethren (Genesis 37:13–14, 18) as Jesus came to his own and his own received him not (John 1:11).
- Joseph's brethren refused and hated him (Genesis 37:8, 18–24) as Jesus was hated without cause (John 15:25, Mark 8:31, John 5:16–18).
- Joseph was envied by his brethren (Genesis 37:11) as the chief priests delivered Jesus for envy (Mark 15:10).
- Joseph was sold by his brethren (Genesis 37:27–28). Jesus was sold by his disciple Judas (Matthew 26:15).
- They conspired against Joseph to slay him (Genesis 37:18). The Jews took council against Jesus to put him to death (Matthew 27:1, John 11:53).
- Joseph was innocent but was accused and condemned (Genesis 39:13–14, 20) as Jesus was falsely condemned to death (Matthew 26:59–60, 65–66).
- Joseph and Jesus were both silent before their accusers (Genesis 39:20, Mark 15:4–5).
- Joseph was placed in prison to show his death (Genesis 39:20). Jesus was buried in the tomb of Joseph of Arimathaea (Matthew 27:57–60).
- Joseph was resurrected from prison, then exalted in Egypt with Pharaoh (Genesis 41:40–42). So Jesus was resurrected and exalted with the Father (Hebrews 8:1, 12:2).

- Joseph had all things put into his hand (Genesis 39:4). As Jesus was given all things into his hand (John 3:35).
- Joseph on the throne of Pharaoh became the provider of bread to starving Egypt (Genesis 41:57). So Jesus on his Father's throne is the "Bread of Life" (John 6:33, 35, 48, 51).
- Joseph knew his brethren when they came to him the first time, but they did not know it was Joseph (Genesis 42:7–8). Jesus knew his brethren when he came the first time, but "they said unto him, Who art thou?" (John 8:25).
- Joseph revealed himself to his brethren when they came the "second time." Jesus will be recognized by the Jews when he comes the second time (Genesis 45:3–4, Zechariah 12:10).
- Joseph was used by God to preserve posterity in the earth and to deliver them by a great deliverance (Genesis 45:7) as Christ will clothe his people in deliverance (1 Chronicles 11:14, Psalms 18:50, Joel 2:32).
- Joseph sends his brethren and their families to the "land of Goshen" (Genesis 45:10). So Jesus will reestablish the Jews in the land of Israel.
- Joseph was a servant (Genesis 40:4) as Jesus came to serve (Luke 22:27).

The life of Joseph clearly parallels the life of Christ. Now, when we get to looking at the marriage of Joseph, all these types add to the shadow of good things to come, and they shine a bright light on a pre-tribulation rapture of the bride of Christ. To argue against this is to do damage to the beauty and harmony of what the Scripture is revealing.

After Joseph was exalted out of prison to the throne of Egypt, he got Asenath, a Gentile bride, during the time of his rejection by his brethren (Genesis 41:45) as Jesus will get his Gentile bride, the church, after his resurrection and during the time of rejection by his brethren (John 1:11).

"After Joseph got his bride his brethren suffered famine and came to him for corn, so after Jesus gets his bride, his brethren, the Jews, will turn to him, during the time of Jacob's trouble, the great tribulation, for relief"3 The famine in Egypt is a picture of (the world), so the type shows a seven-year period of tribulation on the known world of Egypt. This shows a clear type of Gentile bride for Joseph and how he gets his bride before the tribulation on the known world, just as Christ will get his bride before the tribulation on this present world.

It becomes very hard to argue with the flow and harmony of the Scriptures when we look at the types throughout the Bible that only add clear insight for a pre-trib rapture of the church, which is the bride of Christ. It is evident that there are many different types throughout Scripture that help us as believers to know the true meaning of (good things to come). We will see the excellency in these types revealed when we search for them as though they were gold to be discovered. The truth in the Bible is not just found on the surface; it's when we dig for them. It is not just line upon line but also precept upon precept. It is important that we search through all the stories of Jewish ceremonies and feasts so we can find the deeper things of God to understand his intentions and to have the mind of Christ.

Some will still resist the beauty and the excellency of the types found in the Bible that only reveal good things to come. It seems that some people would rather hope for bad things, but the Bible clearly reveals a pre-tribulation rapture for his bride, the church. How could all of these types not be God appointed? The skeptic will stand in silence without an answer that he can apply to these types. These stories should speak volumes to those who have an open mind about types and precepts. We dare not try to belittle the meanings found here in these stories when they are so easily applied. It makes one wonder if some people haven't closed their eyes deliberately to these things. Christians can get a hold of books that sometimes have a violent view of what is going to happen to his church, and then they will start to ignore these beautiful Bible stories. Clearly they were put into the Word of God to help us understand the mysteries, but unto those that are without they are just stories to confound the wise. We dare not want to be people that close the eyes to the beauty and the light that shines through these stories.

- Isaac is seen as a clear type of Christ.

- Isaac and Christ were both children of promise (Genesis 15:4, Isaiah 7:14).
- The births of Isaac and Jesus were foretold before their birth (Genesis 18:10, Luke 1:30–31).
- Both Christ and Isaac were given names before they were born (Genesis 17:19, Luke 1:31).
- Both were born of a miracle: Sarah was barren; Mary was a virgin (Genesis 11:30, Matthew 1:18–20).
- Both Isaac and Christ were called only son (Genesis 22:2, Hebrews 11:17, John 3:16).
- Isaac had not broken the law for which he should be executed (Genesis 22:2, Matthew 27:24).
- "As Isaac carried the wood on which he was to die, so Christ carried his Own Cross" 4 Genesis 22:6, John 19:17).
- Isaac went willingly to the altar, so Christ of his own will went to the cross (Genesis 22:9, John 10:17).
- Both seemed forsaken by their fathers (Genesis 22:2, 9–10, Matthew 27:46).

If Isaac's life so closely parallels that of Christ, then why wouldn't his marriage to Rebekah parallel in some way the marriage of Christ to his bride? This is a fair question for those who have failed to look at these wonderful picture stories. These marriages were to men who clearly were types of Christ in the Old Testament. "For whatsoever things were written aforetime were written for our learning, that we through patience and comfort of the Scriptures might have hope" (Romans 15:4). It is a picture of faith, hope, and love. Even a child can see the beauty of the Lord here in these stories. The truth is ever present in these stories, and the mysteries of the ages are revealed within these stories.

What was the role that Eliezer played, and what does that reveal about Christ and his bride? Eliezer is revealed as a type of the Holy Spirit. Eliezer is seen as the servant of Abraham, sent by Father Abraham to get a bride for his son Isaac and to guide Rebekah, as the Holy Spirit is a servant of God and how he guides us on our path into the presence of our Isaac—Jesus (Genesis 15:1–2, 24:2–4, John 14:26, 15:26).

As Eliezer's mission was to go to Haran to find a bride, so he went to the city of Nahor of Abraham's brethren, to get a bride for Isaac, a picture of the Holy Spirit being sent from heaven to get a bride for Christ (Genesis 24:7–10).

"As Eliezer was not sent to get a bride for Isaac until after he was typically offered up, so the Holy Spirit was not sent to get a bride for Christ until after his death and resurrection" 5

Eliezer spoke only of his master's son, so the Holy Spirit does not talk about himself but testifies of Christ (John 15:26). Eliezer would not be hindered, as the Holy Spirit is urgent (Genesis 24:53–56, 2 Corinthians 6:2). As Eliezer "brought forth jewels of silver, and jewels of gold" and he gives them to Rebekah, he reveals the wealth of his master Isaac. The Holy Spirit enlightens our understanding of the riches of the glory of his inheritance in the saints (Genesis 24:53, Ephesians 1:17–18).

"When Eliezer got Rebekah's consent to be the bride of Isaac he himself took her back; he did not send her back while he remained with her kinsfolk. So when the bride, the church, is ready, the holy spirit will go back to heaven with her" 6 (Hebrews 13:5, Revelation 4:1–5, John 14:16–17).

Rebekah, a beautiful type of the bride of Christ, as seen in her marriage arraignment. As Rebekah was a virgin, so the church will be presented as an espoused virgin to Christ (Genesis 24:16, 2 Corinthians 11:2). Rebekah by faith believed and yielded to the pleadings of Eliezer. This is a picture of the church, and how believers yield to the Holy Spirit (Genesis 24:57–58). By faith Rebekah was willing to separate herself from her family for Isaac's sake. A portrait of how as Christians we must be willing to separate our selves for Jesus sake (Genesis 24:57–58, John 20:29).

Her family proclaimed unto Rebekah, "be thou the mother of thousands of millions, and let thy seed possess the gate of those which hate them" (Genesis 24:60) as the church will prevail over the gates of hell and bring thousands of millions of believers to Christ (Revelation 22:17, Matthew 16:18).

As Eliezer on the journey to Isaac told faithful Rebekah all about Isaac, so the Holy Spirit on our faith-filled earthly journey reveals to us what is in store for the faithful when we meet our Isaac-Jesus (John 16:13–14).

As Rebekah was a Gentile bride, so the church of Christ is a Gentile bride. It is not revealed that Rebekah passed through any tribulation as she left her home to go to Isaac, so the church will not have to pass through any part of the tribulation before meeting Jesus (Revelation 4:1). As Isaac went out into the field to meditate, he then meets Rebekah. So Jesus waits from heaven to meet his bride, a "cloud of witnesses," in the air (Genesis 24:63, 1 Thessalonians 4:16–18, Hebrews 12:1). "As It was "eventide" when Isaac met Rebekah, so it will be the EVENTIDE OF THIS DISPENSATION WHEN JESUS MEETS HIS CHURCH" 7 Genesis 24:63).

As Isaac came from the well of Lahai-roi (Genesis 24:62), which means "the presence of him that liveth and seeth." So Christ will leave his Father's presence who liveth and seeth, to go out and meditate in the field and meet his bride (Genesis 24:62–63, John 17:20–24).

These graceful stories do not reveal that his bride is going through the tribulation; it just isn't revealed. Quite the contrary, it only shows how the church at the end of this dispensation of grace will be met by the Lord himself in the clouds. It's a love story with a glorious ending, and these types in the Bible are a shadow of good things to come. How is it that people who are mid-trib or post-trib have missed all of these precepts? You cannot argue for bad things when the Bible says these things are shadows of good things to come. Not even a whisper of any part of the seven-year tribulation is revealed in these stories. This again only adds to the type with Joseph taking his Gentile bride before the seven-year famine and then Rebekah not going through any tribulation before she is taken. Those who refuse to see the light as it concerns the types have to look away from the light and the beauty that is illuminated here in these stories.

Enoch pictures a clear type of translated or raptured saint. He was raptured before the flood, and the flood is seen as a type of tribulation on the world. Noah and his family would represent the Jewish remnant. The Jewish remnant will be preserved through the seven-year tribulation and then go into the kingdom upon the earth. This echoes how Noah and his family went out again upon the earth after the flood, as the children of Israel will go into the kingdom of heaven upon the earth after the tribulation.

Even Moses at times is seen as a type of Christ as he got a Gentile bride before the plagues and tribulation under Pharaoh (Exodus 2:21–25).

Ruth and Boaz

The story of Ruth, a Gentile, is yet another beautiful type where Boaz is Ruth's kinsman redeemer as Christ is our redeemer. Ruth by faith and because she loved Naomi followed along with her, and Naomi is seen as a type of Israel. Ruth proclaims as a Gentile that "thy people shall be my people, and thy God my God" (Ruth 1:16). Her faith and love for the God of Israel are seen so clearly here. It was her faith and love that caught Boaz' eye, and she bowed herself,

> And said unto him, Why have I found grace in thine eyes, that thou shouldest take knowledge of me, seeing I am a stranger? And Boaz answered and said unto her, It hast fully been shewed me, all that thou hast done unto thy mother in law since the death of thine husband: and how thou hast left father and thy mother, and the land of thy nativity, and art come unto a people which thou knewest not heretofore.
>
> Ruth 2:10–11

Boaz married Ruth as her kinsman redeemer as Christ responds to us in faith and when we are willing to leave all behind for the God of Israel. Ruth, a picture of the church from her conversion to the God of Israel and to marrying Boaz, did not go through tribulation. Ruth is only shown as proclaiming her faith, serving, resting, and being rewarded. A portraiture like unto the followers of Christ and the beauty is, there was no tribulation from whence she first believed. The love of God for his bride is so pictured throughout the Scriptures it is undeniable. Even the name Ruth means friend or friendship. Jesus said to the disciples, "But I have called you friends" (John 15:15).

If we fail to look upon the types in the Bible, we neglect the luster and the beauty that God has presented to us through his Word. The church is pictured as having a lofty place in the Lord reserved for her, and failure to acknowledge this as it's revealed in the types is so tragic because we will miss the mysteries that are revealed in them. Some people will not grasp the true position of the bride of Christ because they have neglected these precepts found in these stories. They are not searching for the deep meanings that are drawn from these types, and they are found all throughout the Bible. The church will rule as consorts in his kingdom, and we will co-share in his reign (John 14:20). Remember in the final standing we are not servants or subjects. The bride (always) reigns with the bridegroom; she is not a subject in the kingdom (John 17:21–26). The bride is never invited to her own wedding. A bride is there at her wedding by her standing in that she is marrying the bridegroom. She will not be a subject in the kingdom; she will rule and reign with Christ!

The church will be raptured just as Enoch was (taken to heaven before the tribulation of the flood began), leaving the remnant of the Jews to go through the tribulation flood but ultimately protected in the ark. As Isaac's Gentile bride Rebekah was met by Isaac in the evening, so will the Lord meet his bride, the church, in the evening of the day of grace and right before the Day of the Lord starts. To the world, it will be like a thief in the night. This event will usher in the Day of the Lord. The Lord will take his bride before the seven-year tribulation just as Joseph took his bride before the seven-year famine.

Moses and the Children of Israel

Moses and the children of Israel were a type of the church. The Lord comes to Moses in a cloud with the voice of a trumpet, and then the people would come up to Mt. Sinai (Exodus 19:13, 16), just like the church when it hears the trumpet and is caught up in the clouds to meet the Lord (Exodus 19:9, 13, 16; 20:18; 1 Corinthians 15:51–53; 1 Thessalonians 4:16–18). Moses and the children of Israel would hear the trumpet and go up to Mt Sinai as the Lord descended in the cloud. Hebrews 12:18–23 connects this thought together with how Israel heard the trumpet and went up to Mt Sinai, but Israel could not endure that which was commanded at Mt Sinai.

The church also hears a trumpet and,

> Are come unto Mount Sion, and unto the city of the living God, the heavenly Jerusalem, and to an innumerable company of angels. To the general assembly and church of the firstborn, which are written in heaven, and to God the Judge of all, and to the spirits of just men made perfect.
>
> Hebrews 12:22–23

So, the trumpet sounding and the going up to Mt. Sinai are similar for the church; but the church will be changed and raised incorruptible (1 Corinthians 15:52–53), and we will receive everything in Mt. Sion, in heaven.

In the Old Testament, Israel was known as the wife of God, albeit an unfaithful wife. But Moses led her out of harm's way when the Lord parted the Red Sea to let her cross over to the promised land and away from Pharaoh and his chariots. How can anyone within the church think that the Lord would do anything less when talking about the bride of Christ? There were those who murmured against Moses in his day, and they said it would have been better to have stayed in Egypt than to die in the wilderness. So for all those who think the church is going to be bloodied and martyred at the water's edge, I would recommend to them what Moses said, "stand still, and see the salvation of the LORD, which he will shew to you to day" (Exodus 14:13). God did not leave his wife at the water's edge to be slaughtered, and neither will he leave the bride of Christ to be slaughtered in the tribulation. As the children of Israel crossed through the Red Sea on dry land, the beloved will be caught up in the air out of this world, through the sheepfold door and into his presence.

A glorious picture of the rapture of the church is seen with the Apostle John. It is seen in Revelation 4:1, where he is clearly seen as a type of the church being translated or raptured to heaven after he hears a trumpet that says to, "come up hither, and I will shew thee things which must be hereafter." You would think even a skeptic would ask, "hereafter what?" Even starting this verse, it says "After this," this follows the church and the conclusion of the messages to the seven churches; this is what it was referring to. From here on the church is no longer seen on earth, as John was then immediately in the Spirit before the throne.

Most evangelicals would agree that this is a picture or type of the rapture of the church, but there is even more in chapter four of Revelation that points to a pre-trib rapture. In verse four the twenty-four elders are now in heaven before the throne. Who are they? They are the Old Testament saints representing the twelve tribes of Israel along with the twelve apostles. Notice they are in heaven before the throne (Revelation 4:4–5, 10–11). This is a clear picture of the rapture, or first resurrection.

In verse five, it also shows the seven spirits of God before the throne. The "seven spirits of God" is a term that shows the completeness or perfectness of. In Isaiah 11:2, it says this concerning the sevenfold spirit. "And the spirit of the LORD shall rest upon him, without measure, the spirit of wisdom and understanding, the spirit of counsel and might, the spirit of knowledge and of the fear of the LORD" (John 3:34). This is an indication that indeed the Holy Spirit's work is completed on the earth for the church age, and now he is seen in heaven having escorted the saints before the throne (John 14:16). Then, the picture of crowns being thrown before the throne only underscores the fact the church is no longer on earth but is now in heaven having received her crowns. This is the only place in the book of Revelation where crowns could have been received. There are no other references to be found for when the church receives crowns!

So, John hears the trumpet and has been caught up to heaven, and he sees the twenty-four elders in heaven and the Holy Spirit now in heaven. This is a clear type for a pre-tribulation rapture of the church. Mid-trib or post-trib views of the rapture won't fit here at all. If John is a type of church being raptured, then what John sees is what we the church will witness during the rest of the book of Revelation. John referred to himself as the disciple whom Jesus loved at least four times in the Gospel of John. If what we are seeing here is in essence a love story of good things to come, then it certainly fits that John, representing a type of the church in Revelation 4:1, is truly the beloved. It shows Jesus' love for his bride in John the beloved. This only fits with the rapture of the church at the start of the tribulation. The Holy Spirit had John point out the love that the Lord had for John the beloved for a distinct reason, to show that we (his bride) will be removed from the earth at the start of Revelation 4. If John is a type of the church, it is noteworthy also that he was the only apostle that was not martyred. Why is that important, because there are those people who assume that the church will be martyred during the tribulation. But, if John is a type of the church (beloved), then the church will not be martyred.

These are all lovely and beautiful types that keep revealing a pre-trib rapture of the church and in John the beloved an actual picture of the church and Old Testament saints, along with the Holy Spirit (our Eliezer), now in heaven and all of this happening by Revelation 4:1–5. The Bible does not reveal a roughed-up bride in any of the stories we've looked at; they only demonstrate the opposite. No one can argue against these beautiful stories and the light they shed. As the angel said to Lot, "Hurry, escape there, for I cannot do anything until you arrive there" (Genesis 19:22, NAS). The angel could not let the judgment start until Lot was safely removed from Sodom and Gomorrah.

The time of judgment and tribulation on the earth cannot start until the church is raptured out of this world; then Daniel's seventieth week can start. It will be a time of purging out the sinners of Israel and judgment on the world to bring in the millennial kingdom. This is when we see the Lamb in Revelation chapter five take the book out of the right hand of the Father because all judgment has been given to the Son. At this point Jesus is no longer sitting on the throne of grace, and judgment is about to begin with the opening of the first seal; then the rider on the white horse who is the antichrist appears.

The church has been ushered into the heavenly balcony, with a front-row seat watching what is to come; we have cast our crowns before the throne to worship the Lord. We shall appear with him in glory (Colossians 3:4). "My beloved spake, and said unto me, Rise up, my love, my fair one, and come away" (Song of Solomon 2:10). The precepts of old are understood when, we view the type with Christ in the lens, the greatest prize awarded, and yet to be found, when we look for gold nuggets, and they're all around.

What imagination do we need
to see within the story of what we read
Graceful silhouettes presented through the gloss and glow
We see them written throughout Scripture,
with the imagery they bestow
We see John the beloved, as the church and sheep entered in
For when his voice they hear, they disappear
Through the sheepfold door they go, leav-
ing this world of wrath to go
Then in the resurrection, the elders are now seen
Receiving their crowns in glory, and conquerors they will be
Then the lamb arises, now as they all sing
For thou hast redeemed us
From every tribe they're from
So when the ten thousand times ten thousand cry worthy
It's only just begun

The Church Age and the Rapture

Many good people who hold different views of the rapture other than pre-trib may have a hard time with this next chapter. From what I have witnessed, there is a real reluctance and even avoidance to talk about these early chapters of the book of Revelation. You'll notice how people can tell you all about pre-wrath or post-trib views, but when it comes to the first five chapters of Revelation they all of sudden would rather move on and talk about all the seals, trumpets and bowls found later in the book of Revelation. We cannot just move on so quickly when there is such an architectural setting up of events found here in the first five chapters of the book of Revelation. They help set up the picture of "which is, and which was, and which is to come." The church age is seen. The typology of John the beloved is seen: the question of, who are the twenty-four elders, and then what does it mean that the Lamb is seen standing? Does this signal that the time of grace has ended, especially as it rolls right into the opening of the first seal? Add to this the direct parallelism of the Gospel of John chapter five with Revelation four and five. Found here are some of the most unshakable themes of the Bible concerning the first resurrection and the authority given to Jesus to judge the earth, mixed in with the twenty-four elders throwing their crowns before the throne. I can only thank the Lord for enlightening me and showing me some of these wonderful truths as they are gold nuggets to me, and it is an absolute honor to be able to share them.

This chapter helps to tell the story and reveals afresh the beauty and evidence for the rapture of the church, which many times is overlooked. It shows that there is a treasure of scriptural support for the rapture of the church coming before the seven-year tribulation. The book of Revelation in chapters four and five have some very enlightening verses in them as it concerns the rapture of the church, the heavenly scene, and the judgment that follows. Most Bible commentaries would agree that chapter three closes out the church age, as it is seen in history. Then to start chapter four, it says, "After this [or after the church age] I looked, and, behold, a door opened in heaven: and the first voice which I heard was as it were of a trumpet talking with me; which said, come up hither, and I will shew thee things which must be hereafter." So after the church age, it is John the beloved who sees what will happen after the church is caught up.

In Revelation 4:1 John the beloved sees a door opened in heaven. Also, in the Gospel of John 10:1, Jesus talks about the door into the sheepfold. Then in verse nine, Jesus says he is the door, and in verse eleven, Jesus says he is the Good Shepherd. It is interesting that it is the same Greek word for door (yura thura) that is used in Revelation 4:1, and it is what John used for the door into the sheepfold in John 10:1. John is caught up through the door into the sheepfold, and John sees everything as a type of the church in chapter four. In John 10:3 Jesus says, "And the sheep hear his voice: and he calleth his own sheep by name, and leadeth them out for they know his voice." John is caught up through the sheepfold door as he hears a voice of a trumpet. This is a beautiful picture of the rapture of the church as it is shown in 1 Corinthians 15:51–52; 1 Thessalonians 4:16–18; Hebrews 12:18–23; Revelation 1:10–11; 4:1.

The word church or churches mysteriously disappears from Revelation after Revelation 3:22 and is not mentioned again until Revelation 22:16–17, and then it only references back to what the angel was going to tell John in the first three chapters concerning "these things in the churches."

> I Jesus have sent mine angel to testify unto you these things in the churches. I am the root and the offspring of David, and the bright and morning star. And the Spirit and the bride say, come. And let him that heareth say,

> Come. And let him that is athirst come. And whosoever will, let him take the water of life freely.
>
> Revelation 22:16–17

The bride will not be in the tribulation but is seen here looking back from glory and beckoning all to come. That is our destiny in the Lord, to be tucked away and observing everything from heaven as John the beloved did. Too many people are trying to put the church into all of the Revelation when the truth before you is; the church is not even mentioned or seen on earth during the seven seals of judgment.

John the Beloved

The Holy Spirit used the Apostle John to write the Gospel of John, but he would later use John again to write the book of Revelation. When the Apostle John writes his gospel, he makes a very curious statement, and to many people this statement is overlooked and doesn't really mean anything; but we know that every jot and tittle means something in God's Word. It's found in the repeated phrase, "The disciple whom Jesus loved," repeated to show its importance, and it's found at least four times in the Gospel of John. Why would he use that term, and why would the Holy Spirit include that about John in the text? Unless, John would later write the book of Revelation, and he would typify the church being caught up through the sheepfold door and raptured to heaven in the spirit! In the heart of God, John is the beloved. John is also known as John the divine, which seems to point to divine love as much as it points to his inspired writings. Some people will scoff at the idea of the Apostle John being cast as a type of raptured church in Revelation 4, but they have to ignore all the signs and drive right around a mountain of evidence that shows that is exactly how he is portrayed.

There is no record of John the beloved being martyred; in typology this once again points to John as the espoused beloved.

Another intriguing example that hints at the church is found when we read:

> Then Peter, turning about, seeth the disciple whom Jesus loved following; which also leaned on his breast at supper, and said, Lord, which is he that betrayeth thee? Peter seeing him saith to Jesus, Lord, and what shall this man do? Jesus saith unto him, If I will that he tarry till I come, what is that to thee? Follow thou me. Then went this saying abroad among the brethren, that that disciple should not die: yet Jesus said not unto him, He shall not die; but, If I will that he tarry till I come, what is that to thee?
>
> John 21:20–23

The Scriptures have this unusual reference here in the book of John as it relates to John (the disciple whom Jesus loved) not dying, but Jesus wasn't saying that John would not die.

The only other explanation is again found in the typology of John, a picture of the church not dying. Jesus wasn't referring to John specifically, but this reference leaves the door open for the beloved not dying. And that is what the brethren thought about John, but it was more a reference for the church in the future. It's just that John signifies the church. It's very hard to describe this portion of Scripture in any other way other than in the light of John the beloved typifying the church in the future. Jesus allowed it because he wasn't referring to John not dying; no, it was about his church one day in the future. This was not a picture of confusion but rather a foreshadowing of the church presented to us about the beloved. What a magnificent picture this is; it's a scene of his church still on earth when he calls his bride and those not seeing death. Remember, that is what the brethren thought about John, so it's safe for us to have the same thoughts about his church

The Twenty-four Elders

John immediately sees the throne in heaven; he then describes the appearance of him who sat upon the throne like jasper and a sardine stone. And there was a rainbow round about the throne, in sight like unto an emerald. "And round about the throne were four and twenty seats: and upon the seats I saw four and twenty elders sitting, clothed in white raiment; and they had on their heads crowns of gold" (Revelation 4:4). The question becomes, who are the twenty-four elders? The twelve gates had names written on them, which represent the twelve tribes of Israel, Old Testament saints (Revelation 21:12). In verse fourteen it says, "The wall of the city had twelve foundations, and in them the names of the twelve apostles of the Lamb" the New Testament saints. (Revelation 21:14).

Jesus tells the apostles that they would sit on twelve thrones judging the twelve tribes of Israel. (Matthew 19:27–28, Luke 22:30). The Old Testament saints are also included when we read in Psalms, "For there are set thrones of Judgment, the thrones of the house of David" (Psalm 122:5). In Deuteronomy 16:18 we see again that there were to be judges in all thy gates. Jesus addresses the disciples, and he told them they would sit on twelve thrones judging the twelve tribes of Israel. In Revelation 20:4 right after Satan is bound for a thousand years, we see thrones, and judgment was given unto them. This is the judgment of the nations to set up the millennial kingdom upon the earth, and it further shows that the apostles are part of the twenty-four elders.

The twenty-four elders also represent the first resurrection or (harvest) as it took place back in Revelation 4–5. The twenty-four elders in Revelation are always seen in heaven until the judgment of the nations (Revelation 20:4).

We must take a momentary side trail here because we are talking about the first resurrection, and it mentions it in Revelation 20:4–6. These tribulation saints have a part, or share, in the first resurrection. This is a beautiful picture of the Feast of Tabernacles or (temporary shelter) for seven days, or one week (Deuteronomy 16:13–15, Leviticus 19:9–10). This shows that the gleanings follow at the end of the harvest. It tells us that the first resurrection, or harvest, isn't over completely until the gleanings of the tribulation saints are brought in one week after. These are those who received not the mark.

The Tabernacles Feast of Booths, Sukkot, or Feast of

Ingathering would last seven days after the harvest was brought in. 8 It was a festival of white-robed priests. The children of Israel would rejoice and sing songs and especially the Hallel Psalms of 113 to 118, with the Messianic words of Psalms 118:25–26. "Save now, I beseech Thee, O Lord: O Lord, I beseech thee, send now prosperity. Blessed be he that cometh in the name of the Lord." On the seventh day, called "Hoshana Rabbah," which means "The Great Salvation," the priests circled the altar seven times. They would chant the Hallel Psalm: "Save now, I beseech Thee, O Lord." This is a marvelous picture as it relates to the tribulation saints who are martyred, where they cry, "How long O Lord!" (Revelation 6:9–10). They also have palm branches in their hands, which are used during the Feast of Tabernacles, and it further illustrates that the martyred saints are not part of the main harvest but follow within the seven day Feast of Tabernacles. The Hallel Psalms in 116:15 includes, "Precious in the sight of the Lord is the death of his saints." This substantiates the timing, and it pictures the tribulation saints within the Halell Psalms. They are now clearly seen within this seven-day Feast of Tabernacles. The church is already caught up into glory in heaven, but these souls of the martyrs have to wait seven years. They are the (gleanings of the harvest). "But the rest of the dead lived not again until the thousand years were finished" (Revelation 20:5–6).

Jesus did not mention to the disciples, the other twelve elders, because they will represent the Old Testament saints. By not mentioning them to his twelve disciples, he shows that the two groups are not the same, but they are all seen in heaven in Revelation 4. It is interesting that these elders in Revelation 4 are not just sitting on thrones, but they have received crowns! This shows that the church has been caught up to heaven and we have received our rewards. "And when the chief Shepherd shall appear, ye shall receive a crown of glory that fadeth not away" (1 Peter 5:4).

We know that we will all stand before the judgment seat of Christ to receive our rewards (2 Corinthians 5:10). The apostles will stand before the judgment seat of Christ right along with the rest of the church. The twenty-four elders in heaven are a picture of the first resurrection, with the Old Testament saints and the church represented. The tribulation saints with their temporary shelter of seven days, or one week, to follow at the end of the tribulation in Revelation 20:4–5, bringing to a close the Feast of Tabernacles week. But here in Revelation 4, we will all fall down and worship the Lord in Spirit and in truth and cast our crowns before the throne!

There isn't another explanation of who these twenty-four elders are, other than the saints of the Old Testament and the church of the New Testament, with the apostles named as sitting on twelve thrones. There are no creatures in the Bible that have crowns (like the church) that are given thrones to sit on (other than the apostles) that we see here. They are included with the other elders who represent the resurrected saints of the Old Testament. Without us they would not be made perfect (Hebrews 11:39–40). One cannot find another reference for when the church receives crowns in the book of Revelation other than this scene of the twenty-four elders before the throne, and it comes before the opening of the first seal.

The Wycliffe Bible early translation used the phrase elder men six times when referring to the twenty-four elders in Revelation 4–5. Even William Tyndale used the term, "seniours syttinge clothed in whyte rayment, and had on their heddes crounes of gold." In the Geneva Bible of 1560, the elders are clearly understood to be men. The footnote in the Geneva Bible says, "Our Sauior Iefus hathe redemed his church by his blood sheding and gathered it of all nations." With all of the early translations of the Bible, there was no uncertainty as to who were redeemed by his blood or that the twenty-four elders were redeemed men. Even Matthew Henry in 1706 comments on how the twenty-four elders represented the saints. Sadly, it is only in the later translations we see that men have changed the wording to now muddy the waters about the twenty-four elders. The footnote in the NIV gets it right when it says, "the twenty-four elders in this vision probably represent all the redeemed of God for all time (both before and after Christ's death and resurrection). They symbolize all those Jews and Gentiles who are now part of God's family." 9 Adding to all this is the fact that even the artwork of two hundred to over three hundred years ago when depicting the twenty-four elders showed pictures of men in them. Now where did they get such ideas? It was from the earlier translations of the Bible, not the later, liberal versions that left out whole passages and changed thousands of words.

The twenty-four elders are further identified in Revelation 5:8–10. It says,

> And when he had taken the book… four and twenty elders fell down before the Lamb, having every one of them harps, and golden vials full of odours, which are the prayers of saints. And they sung a new song, saying, Thou art worthy to take the book, and to open the

> seals thereof: for thou wast slain, and hast redeemed us to God by thy blood out of every kindred, and tongue, and people, and nation. And hast made us unto our God kings and priests: and we shall reign on the earth.
>
> Revelation 5:8–10

This is a clear picture of the church, for there can be no other group redeemed from mankind by his blood from every people and tongue. Some people have falsely tried to say that the twenty-four elders are angels, but that cannot be true because Jesus died to redeem men, not angels. This is also a repeated phrase from Revelation 1:5–6, which is clearly the church, as John was addressing the church. They repeat the same phrase again in Revelation 5:9–10 as they do in Revelation 1:5–6, but now they are seen in heaven, and this is all before the Lamb even opens the book to start Revelation 6.

The Lamb Stands to Take the Book

In Revelation 5, John wept when he realized that no one was worthy to open the book to read it or even look upon it. Revelation 5:5 says, "And one of the elders saith unto me, weep not: the Lion of the tribe of Juda, the Root of David, hath prevailed to open the book, and to loose the seven seals thereof. And I beheld, and, lo, in the midst of the throne ... stood a lamb." Things in heaven and earth have changed; the rapture has taken place! The scene in heaven is changing; the judgment of the book of Revelation is about to be set in motion! In the book of Hebrews 4:16, it says, "Let us therefore come boldly unto the throne of grace, that we may obtain mercy, and find grace to help in time of need." See also Colossians 3:1, "where Christ sitteth on the right hand of God." What we are seeing here is the end of the time of grace. The dispensation of grace has ended, and the Lamb has stood up. No one can come unto the throne of grace any longer because the Lamb has stood up to judge the earth; the church age is over, and the elders have received their crowns. Isaiah 3:13 says, "The Lord standeth up to plead, and standeth to judge the people." Revelation 5:7 reveals, "And he came and took the book out of the right hand of him that sat on the throne." He has now received authority from the Father to judge the earth.

Jesus sits on the throne of grace during the church age right now (Hebrews 4:16, Colossians 3:1). Then all of a sudden, the Lamb is seen standing up in Revelation 5:6. This explains the Scriptures that show the Lord arising to shake the earth (Isaiah 2:19, 21; 3:13). These Scriptures are tied directly to Revelation 6:16–17, and they repeat the same thing concerning judgment and men going into the rocks of the cliffs. The Lamb receives authority to judge in Revelation 5:7. It is only after the seven years, or Daniel's seventieth week, that we see Jesus sitting again, and then he is seen sitting on the throne of his glory at the judgment of the nations at the end of tribulation (Matthew 25:31–32, 41). During the great white-throne judgment, he is sitting also (Revelation 20:11). It appears that the only time we see the Lord stand up is during the seven-year tribulation (Psalms 82:1, 8). The Lamb standing and opening the seals in Revelation 6 is also foreboding because it shows where the vengeance of our God starts (Job 19:25; Psalm 94:1–2; Zephaniah 3:8; Zechariah 2:13; 14:4).

Gospel of John Parallels Revelation

There are many common phrases and precepts that flow between the Gospel of John and the book of Revelation. The Gospel of John in chapter five especially seems to have a number of parallel thoughts. The chapter starts with Jesus healing the man at the pool of Bethesda on the Sabbath and then the Jews seeking to kill Jesus. The rest of John 5:19 to the end is Jesus telling the Jews of the resurrections, who he is, and what would happen to the Jewish nation. With this in mind, let's look at John chapter five against Revelation four and five; watch how these same thoughts go between the books.

John 5:22 says, "For the Father judgeth no man, but hath committed all judgment unto the Son." Then in Revelation 5:6, the Lamb stands up to start judgment. The Lamb is no longer sitting on the throne of grace (Hebrews 4:16). Notice how this precept concerns judgment, and it is linked between the two books and within the same placement in each book.

John 5:27 says, "And hath given him authority to execute judgment also, because he is the Son of man." (Revelation 5:7 shows that the Lamb comes and takes the book out of the right hand of him who sits upon the throne, showing that he has now received the authority to judge.) Clearly, this parallel goes between both books, and the theme here is so monumental because it shows the close of the dispensation of grace and the starting of judgment for the seven-year tribulation.

Even the first resurrection is mentioned in John 5:25. "Verily, verily I say unto you, The hour is coming, and now is, when the dead shall hear the voice of the Son of God: and they that hear shall live." In Revelation 4:1 John is caught up to heaven through the Sheepfold Door. The scene in heaven then shows the twenty-four elders throwing their crowns before the throne, indicating the first resurrection. Revelation 4:1 through Revelation 5 shows the church now in heaven falling down before the throne, those who have been redeemed to God by his blood.

In John 5:19 to the end of the chapter, Jesus is putting the Jews in their place. He then says to the Jews in John 5:39, "Search the Scriptures; for in them ye think ye have eternal life: and they are they which testify of me." Then, in verse forty Jesus says something rather startling when he says to the Jews, "And ye will not come to me, that ye might have life" (John 5:40). The importance of this statement as it parallels Revelation 5 is the fact that the Jews have rejected Jesus and the next thing coming is the Revelation scene of judgment, when the Lamb opens the first seal to start Revelation chapter six.

Then another remarkable statement is made by Jesus to the Jews, "But I know you, that ye have not the love of God in you" (John 5:42). Because of the Jews' rejection of Jesus and that they have not the love of God in them, Jesus tells them the consequences. Watch how this again parallels between the two books.

Jesus says, "I am come in my Father's name and ye receive me not: If another shall come in his own name, him ye will receive" (John 5:43). Care to imagine what the very next thing to happen in Revelation is as it parallels the Gospel of John? Enter the four horseman of the apocalypse, the first one being the rider on the white horse. Jesus warned the Jews of the coming consequences of

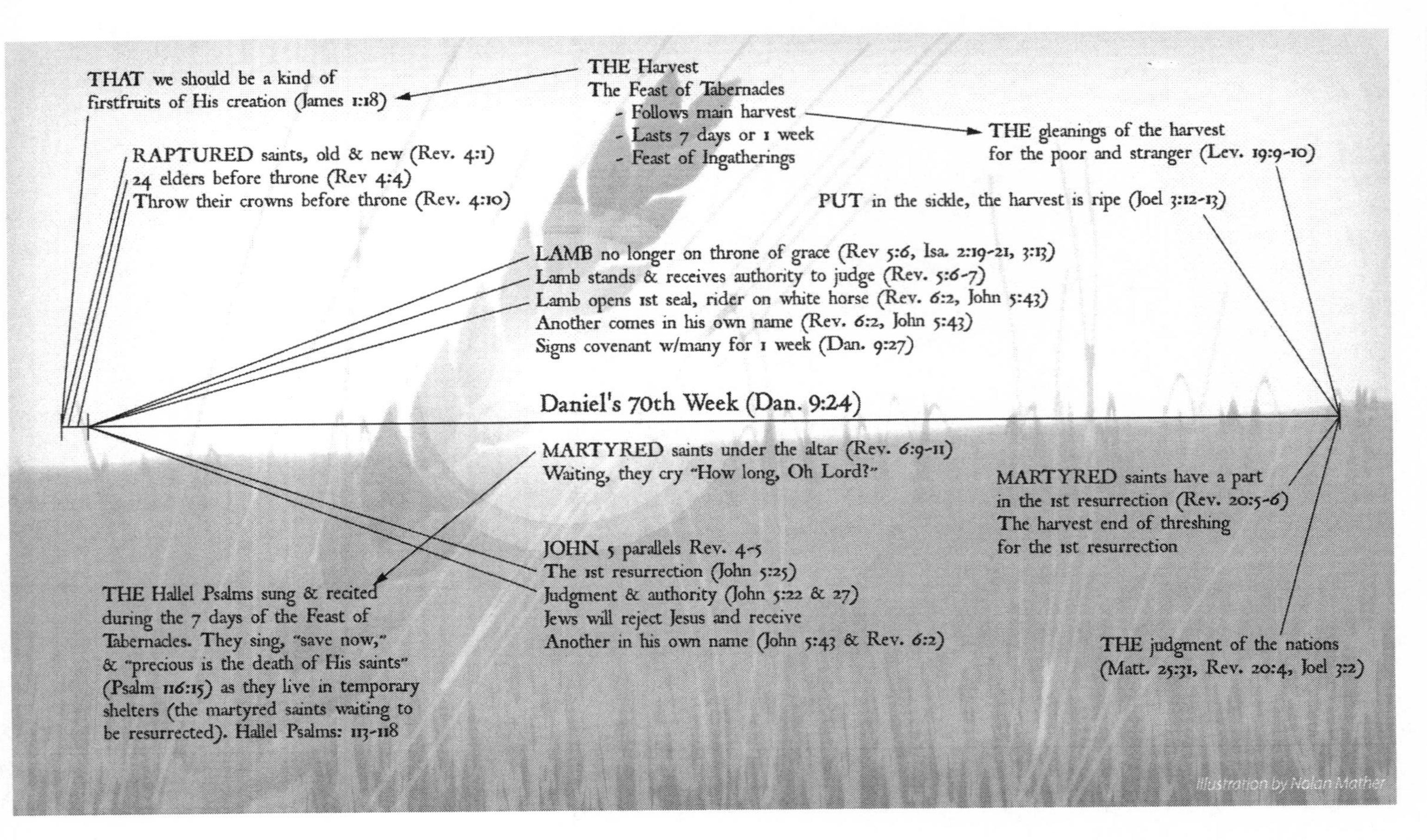
THAT we should be a kind of
firstfruits of His creation (James 1:18)
THE Harvest
The Feast of Tabernacles
- Follows main harvest
- Lasts 7 days or 1 week
- Feast of Ingatherings
THE gleanings of the harvest
for the poor and stranger (Lev. 19:9-10)
RAPTURED saints, old & new (Rev. 4:1)
24 elders before throne (Rev 4:4)
Throw their crowns before throne (Rev. 4:10)
PUT in the sickle, the harvest is ripe (Joel 3:12-13)
LAMB no longer on throne of grace (Rev 5:6, Isa. 2:19-21, 3:13)
Lamb stands & receives authority to judge (Rev. 5:6-7)
Lamb opens 1st seal, rider on white horse (Rev. 6:2, John 5:43)
Another comes in his own name (Rev. 6:2, John 5:43)
Signs covenant w/many for 1 week (Dan. 9:27)
Daniel's 70th Week (Dan. 9:24)
MARTYRED saints under the altar (Rev. 6:9-11)
Waiting, they cry "How long, Oh Lord?"
MARTYRED saints have a part
in the 1st resurrection (Rev. 20:5-6)
The harvest end of threshing
for the 1st resurrection
JOHN 5 parallels Rev. 4-5
The 1st resurrection (John 5:25)
Judgment & authority (John 5:22 & 27)
Jews will reject Jesus and receive
Another in his own name (John 5:43 & Rev. 6:2)
THE Hallel Psalms sung & recited
during the 7 days of the Feast of
Tabernacles. They sing, "save now,"
& "precious is the death of His saints"
(Psalm 116:15) as they live in temporary
shelters (the martyred saints waiting to
be resurrected). Hallel Psalms: 113-118
THE judgment of the nations
(Matt. 25:31, Rev. 20:4, Joel 3:2)
Illustration by Nolan Mather

rejecting him. The rider on the white horse went forth conquering and to conquer. This is the antichrist who the Jews will sign the covenant of death with (Isaiah 28:18) and he who "shall confirm the covenant with many for one week; and in the midst of the week he shall cause the sacrifice and the oblation to cease" (Daniel 9:27, Revelation 13:5). Notice how the church with the twenty-four elders are already in heaven before the throne worshiping, before the Lamb even opens the first seal.

In Revelation 1:5–6 John addresses the church and how we are washed from our sins by his own blood. This letter was sent out to the churches in Asia, the present church at that time. Then in Revelation 1:6 John proclaims that the church has been made kings and priests. Again, this is said about the existing church at that time. Revelation 2–3 shows the church age with the letters to all the churches, and to start Revelation 4 John says after this, meaning after the church age is over these things will follow.

In Revelation 4 John the beloved is raptured, or caught up in the spirit to heaven, through the door into the sheepfold. The same Greek word is used for door in (Revelation 4:1 and John 10:1, 10:9), and Jesus is that door. John the beloved is seen as a type of the church, and he sees what the church will see throughout the Revelation as it unfolds. He sees the throne in heaven (Revelation 4:2, 4, 6), lightnings and thundering, and a sea of glass like crystal. He sees the twenty-four elders sitting on thrones, clothed in white with crowns of gold on their heads (Revelation 4:4). This is the first resurrection. Old and New Testament saints are before the throne. He sees the twenty-four elders, having received their rewards and crowns, fall down and cast their crowns before the throne (Revelation 4:10). This means that judgment of believers has come to pass. John weeps that no one was found worthy to open the book until one of the elders tells him to weep not (Revelation 5:5).

The Lamb stands, and the time of grace has ended. Jesus is no longer sitting upon the throne of grace (Revelation 5:6, Hebrews 4:16, Colossians 3:1). This confirms that the church is in heaven and the dispensation of grace has ended. This signals that judgment is about to start on earth with the opening of the seals. All judgment has been given to the Son (John 5:22).

The Lamb takes the book out of the right hand of him (the Father) who sits upon the throne. Jesus has now received authority to execute judgment (Revelation 5:7, John 5:27): "And hath given him authority to execute Judgment." This awesome scene in heaven goes from rapture to rewards to the vengeance of our God about to begin as the four horsemen start Revelation 6. The twenty-four elders fall down again with harps and vials; these are the believers of the first resurrection.

The raptured saints sing a new song (Revelation 5:9). They proclaim that they have been redeemed by his blood from every kindred and tongue and people and nation. This can only be the church in heaven as there are more than twenty-four countries and tongues and nations redeemed by his blood; this is what was already mentioned by John in Revelation 1:5 concerning the churches but now they are in heaven (Revelation 5:9).

These believers also proclaim that he hath "Made us unto our God, kings and priests" (Revelation 5:10), as John had mentioned concerning the church in Revelation 1:6. John shows the church before the fact on earth in Revelation 1:6 and then in heaven (Revelation 5:10). Speaking to the Jews, Jesus says, "And ye will not come to me, that ye might have life" (John 5:40). "But I know you, that ye have not the love of God in you" (John 5:42). Revelation 5:12 shows the Lamb is preparing to open the first seal because of the Jews rejection. The resurrected saints fall down and worshiped him that liveth forever and ever.

Then we see the consequences of their rejection."If another shall come in his own name, him ye will receive" (John 5:43). In Revelation 6:1–2 the Lamb opens the first seal and behold a white horse! The antichrist goes forth to deceive and make a covenant with many, a covenant of death for the Jews. He comes in his own name, a clear picture that the seven-year tribulation has begun, and the church is in heaven round about the throne.

Summary of Thoughts

- John proclaims the church blood washed (Revelation 1:5)
- John proclaims church kings and priests (Revelation 1:6)

- Will be kept from hour of temptation upon the earth (Revelation 3:10)
- The church age (Revelation 2–3)
- After this or after the church (Revelation 4:1)
- The beloved raptured (Revelation 4:1)
- Things which must be hereafter (Revelation 4:1)
- Heavenly scene (Revelation 4:2)
- He sees the throne in heaven (Revelation 4:2)
- First resurrection, or harvest (John 5:25, Revelation 4:1–4)
- Gleanings of harvest follow (seven days later = seven years) (Revelation 20:4–6, Deuteronomy 16:13, Leviticus 19:9)
- Received their crowns (Revelation 4:4)
- Cast their crowns (Revelation 4:10), fulfilling (1 Peter 5:4, 1 Corinthians 3:12–14)
- No one worthy but the Lamb (Revelation 5:3–5)
- All judgment given unto the Son (John 5:22, Revelation 5:6–7)
- Lamb stands, grace has ended (Revelation 5:6; Hebrews 4:16; Colossians 3:1; Isaiah 3:13; 2:19, 21) men hide in the rocks of the mountains Revelation 6:15–17
- Lamb takes book, now has authority to execute justice (Revelation 5:7, John 5:27)
- The redeemed fall down, having harps and golden vials (Revelation 5:8, John 4:23–24)
- Church redeemed by the blood from every kindred, tongue, people and nation (Revelation 5:9), fulfilling (Revelation 1:5)
- Church proclaims we are made kings and priests (Revelation 5:10), fulfilling Revelation 1:6
- Jews will not come to Jesus for life (John 5:39–41)
- Jesus came in his Father's name (John 5:43)

- If another comes in his own name, him they will receive (John 5:43, Revelation 6:2)
- The Lamb opens the first seal (Revelation 6:1)
- The rider on the white horse (Revelation 6:2)
- He will make a covenant with many for one week (Daniel 9:27)

These are for the most part precepts that come out of Revelation chapters one through six and John 5. These are all pre-trib concepts that we can see; even the gleanings at the end of the harvest after seven days are strong support. The fact that the Gospel of John is at times paralleling the same concepts and thoughts with the book of Revelation adds even more biblical evidence. *Jesus stood up* and said,

> The Spirit of the Lord is upon me, because he hath anointed me to preach the gospel to the poor; he hath sent me to heal the brokenhearted, to preach deliverance to the captives, and recovering of sight to the blind, to set at liberty them that are bruised, To preach the acceptable year of the Lord. And he closed the book.
>
> Luke 4:18–20

Then *Jesus sat down*; he was quoting from Isaiah 61:1–2. Jesus stopped before he read, "And the day of vengeance of our God." The next time Jesus the Lamb stands it will start judgment, when he opens the book in Revelation 6:1. The church is clearly in heaven worshiping the Lord and watching this all unfold as John the beloved did.

The seven seals start the vengeance of our God in Revelation 6 and continue to chapter eight with the first six seals being completed. The seventh seal has all the other judgments in it, and it is seen as going to Revelation 20:4. This is also what Jesus was talking about when he told his disciples that they would sit on thrones, judging the twelve tribes of Israel. This is the judgment of the nations and the setting up of the millennial kingdom. The martyred saints of Revelation are now brought in and included as the gleanings at the end of the harvest of man as they have a part in the first resurrection. "But the rest lived not again until the thousand years were finished. This is the first resurrection" (Revelation 20:5).

"Now in the resurrection, the elders are now seen, receiving their crowns in glory and conquerers they will be. Then the lamb arises, now as they all sing, for thou hast redeemed us, from every tribe they're from. So when the ten thousand times ten thousand cry worthy, it's only just begun."

The martyred saints take the plunge
Into the week of Daniel, with nowhere to run
Having missed the glorious rapture, they are now delayed
These saints must linger as they pray
Crying out for vengeance, to why they died
saying, "How long, O Lord," until they rise
The harvest on earth where men won't kneel,
the Jew, and Gentile the Lord will deal
Within in the harvest scene so real;
The seventy and seventy now revealed
When the church disappeared
Though in mystery to begin the end
Oh, a kind of first fruits bring.

The Martyred Saints and the Harvest

The martyred saints in the book of Revelation are thought by some to really bolster a pre-wrath or post-trib position. But there are times when studying the Bible that the Lord can take something obscure and turn it right back around and it helps send the light so we can understand another portion of Scripture. In the study of Revelation 4–5, I thought I had run into a wall when I realized that the martyrs mentioned in Revelation 20:4–5 have a part in the first resurrection. One might jump to the conclusion that this in someway proves that Christians will be martyred. Not so fast. This only shows that the martyrs have a part in the first resurrection.

What if all of this is a beautiful image of the Feast of the Tabernacles. What a picture it is; first you have within autumn's glow the harvest and (then) you have the seven days of the feast with the Jews looking ahead with their palm branches, and this is seen coming (after) the harvest. The symbolism here is too real to pass off as not being worthy of our full attention. Actually, the martyrs in the tribulation only add to the evidence for a pre-trib rapture of the church. Once you see the picture of the Feast of Tabernacles and see how easily the martyrs of Revelation fit into it, there's no going back. No other view can reconcile the martyrs of Revelation other than pre-trib view as it is brought to light through the Feast of Tabernacles. It seems to be the only way you can understand the end-of-the-age harvest picture.

So, how does this end-of-the-age harvest fit into the book of Revelation? The harvest picture is revealed in the Feast of Tabernacles, which the Jews celebrated at the end of the harvest season. Many people have never considered the Feast of

Tabernacles when discussing Revelation, especially as it pertains to the martyred saints. Jesus' disciples asked, "What shall be the sign of thy coming, and the end of the [age]?" (Matthew 24:3). Jesus said "the harvest is the end of the [age]" (Matthew 13:39). The Jews celebrate the Feast of Tabernacles at the end of the harvest, or growing season, and it commemorates the deliverance of God's people from Egypt and their journey through the wilderness. This is the time when they dwelt in tents and booths, or temporary shelters. During this one-week feast they recite the Halell Psalms of 113 to 118, proclaiming, "Blessed is he who comes in the name of the LORD!" While examining this harvest scene, keep in mind the Scriptures in Revelation that talk about the martyred saints, what they are to wear, and what they have in their hands, and even what they say. Notice how they have to wait seven years and how this runs parallel to the Feast of Tabernacles, where they wait seven days. The imagery found here in this feast at the end of the harvest reveals the entirety of the first resurrection.

People will ask, "What does the Feast of Tabernacles have to do with the book of Revelation?" The answer is the harvest of man is the end of the age, so then let's pay attention to what the Jews do during the Feast of Tabernacles, which concludes the harvest season. In the book of Revelation, it is seen now as the harvest of man and is drawn out over the seven years. If the harvest is the end of the age, then we should have some insight into what the Feast of Tabernacles is showing, like Daniel's seventieth week. Imagine a big grid laid out a certain way and then imagine another grid being laid out over the top of the first one, and you see how it matches in almost every detail. This is what happens when you see what the Jews do during the harvest feast, and then you realize that the martyred saints seen in Revelation are seen doing the same things; they are mirrored in the book of Revelation. Keep this grid picture in your mind's eye as we examine this feast.

The names for the Sukkot, or booths, are the Feast of Tabernacles, the Feast of the Lord, the Feast of Ingathering, the Feast of Booths. These are all pointing to the same feast, the Feast of Tabernacles. Scriptures are Leviticus 23:34; Deuteronomy 16:13–15; 31:10; 2 Chronicles 8:13; Ezra 3:4; Zechariah 14:16–19).

> Also in the fifteenth day of the seventh month, when ye have gathered in the fruit of the land, ye shall keep a feast unto the LORD seven days: on the first day shall be a Sabbath, and on the eight day a Sabbath. And ye shall take you on the first day the boughs of goodly trees, branches of palm trees, and the boughs of thick trees, and willows of brook; and ye shall rejoice before the LORD your God seven days... Ye shall dwell in booths seven days; all that are Israelites born shall dwell in booths.
>
> Leviticus 23:39–42

Some people will argue that the Feast of Tabernacles is eight days, but clearly the Lord says it is to last only seven days. The eighth day, atzeret, is seen as starting something new, as a new growing season or a new beginning, or a time such as the millennium.

There is a distinction to be made here between The Feast of Weeks at Pentecost with the first fruits of the barley offering fifty days after Passover, and the Feast of Tabernacles or Feast of Ingatherings at the end of the growing season in the fall. "And thou shalt observe the Feast of Weeks, of the first fruits of wheat harvest, and the Feast of Ingathering at the year's end." They are two different Jewish festivals (Exodus 34:22).

The Feast of Tabernacles is to commemorate what the Israelites went through coming out of Egypt and how they dwelt in booths and temporary shelters. This feast also looks ahead prophetically into the future with the Jews still looking for Messiah, and it also includes the Gentile nations. "And it shall come to pass, that every one that is left of all the nations which came against Jerusalem shall even go up from year to year to worship the King, the LORD of hosts, and to keep the Feast of Tabernacles" (Zechariah 14:16). This is a clear picture of what will happen even into the millennium with the Gentile nations. There will be consequences for not obeying this feast during the millennium for the nations left on earth. It has nothing to do with the church in heaven. The point is this is a look ahead at what the feast means, even for the Gentiles into the future. The Jews dress up mostly in white robes and make temporary booths, or temporary shelters, from palm branches and dwell in them seven days.

The main harvest happens right before this feast begins, but the harvest is not over entirely until the close of the seventh day. This helps explain the harvest of this age (as the church disappears at the beginning of the Feast) and the gleanings that are left for the poor, and foreigners now reflect (the martyrs) as it's spread over the entire seven days; and in the book of Revelation it is spread over seven years.

Following the seven days, there was to be a holy convocation on the eighth day called atzeret. it was to be a day of abstinence and soberness, and it brought to close the time of harvest; but it also looks ahead to a new beginning, or agricultural cycle (Leviticus 23:36). This is where some Bible scholars point to the millennial kingdom being set up at this time. This would make sense because the number eight means a new beginning. This eighth day begins to look ahead into the kingdom age of the millennium. Leprosy, a picture of sin, was cleansed on the eighth day (Leviticus 14:10–11, 23). This is a picture of the atzeret, but it followed the Feast of Tabernacles and is separate. It's a picture of the Jews being cleansed to bring in the start of the kingdom of heaven on earth (Jeremiah 32:37–41).

There is much to say about the Jews' celebration of the Feast of Tabernacles. Israel would recite the Hallel Psalms 113 to 118 during the Feast of Tabernacles. In Psalms 118:25, it shows the expectation of the Jews for their Messiah to come and save them. This is highly suggestive due to the harvest being the end of the age and this feast of seven days following the harvest. Jesus gave us a clue when he said, "For I say unto you, Ye shall not see me henceforth, till ye shall say, Blessed is he that cometh in the name of the Lord" (Matthew 23:39). We must take a genuine look at this Feast of Sukkot, the Feast of Tabernacles, and what it is revealing.

It is astounding to realize that there is a place in the Bible where it says something about the death of the Lord's saints. It says, "Precious in the sight of the Lord is the death of his saints" (Psalm 116:15). This places the martyrs now squarely within the Hallel Psalms during the Feast of Tabernacles! As suggested, if this harvest festival parallels the end of the age, then we have some interesting features of the feast to look at as it concerns the martyrs in the book of Revelation. In other words, if the rapture has happened in Revelation 4:1 and it represented the main harvest, this then shines a bright light on who these martyred saints are, as they are seen through the eyes of this autumn feast. It helps us get a better picture as to what is going to happen throughout Revelation, as it's revealed through the Jewish festival.

We now have some major themes happening that tie together. The harvest happens first; then the martyred saints are seen waiting within the seven days of the Feast of Tabernacles, or seven years as it is seen in the book of Revelation. They are in temporary shelters under the altar waiting for the Lord to resurrect them, as the Jews are in temporary shelters looking for Messiah at the end of their Feast of Tabernacles. Psalm 116:15 puts the martyrs into this feast because the Hallel Psalms are recited during the Feast of Tabernacles. Daniel's seventieth week is a period of seven years, as the Feast of Tabernacles' seven days now changes to seven years, as seen in the book of Revelation. All of this lines up in sequence with this Feast of Ingatherings as it concerns the harvest. The Revelation martyrs are seen clearly within the Halell Psalms and the end of the age. All of this is revealed in the Feast of Tabernacles.

The Seventieth Week and the Seventy Bulls

There were seventy bulls sacrificed during the Sukkot, and rabbis to this day will tell you that it represents sacrifices for the nations, seventy being a number for the nations (Genesis 10, Numbers 29:12–38). Some Jewish sources say that world redemption is a major theme of the Feast of Tabernacles. In the tribulation, or Daniel's seventieth week, there will be people from all across the world who will not take the mark; this shows how the Gentiles are included into God's plans. They will be martyred and will have temporary shelter under the altar of the Almighty during Daniel's seventieth week (Revelation 6:9–11).

Isn't it ironic that the seventieth week of Daniel has to do with God dealing with the Jewish nation, and the number seventy has to do with the nations, and the seventy sacrificed bulls are for those nations during the Feast of Tabernacles. It is the Jews and

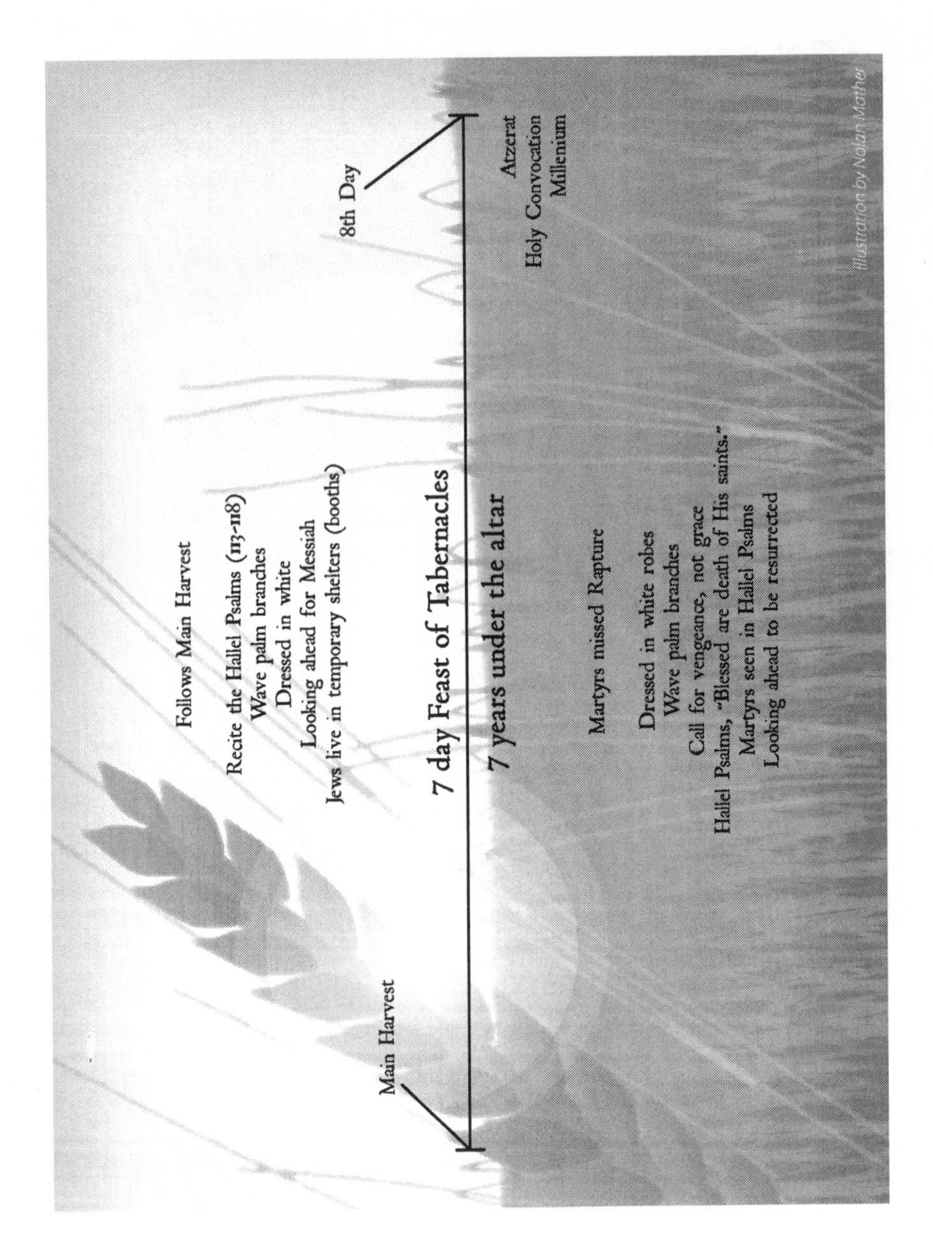

the Gentiles that are being dealt with during the harvest of man as seen in the book of Revelation.

The Lord is working out his plan of salvation for the Jews and the Gentiles *after* the main harvest. Notice how the church is missing in this picture of the Feast of Tabernacles? The picture of the church isn't revealed here because we were the main harvest that preceded the seven-day Feast of Tabernacles. John *the beloved* was taken up to heaven way back in Revelation 4:1 in the main harvest, and John is a clear picture of the church. For the doubters who want to insist that the church is martyred, John the beloved was not martyred. This shows you the harvest picture in the feast. The harvest picture demands that there was a harvest first and then God deals with the Jews and the Gentiles as pictured in the seven days of the Feast of Tabernacles, the harvest of man.

When the Israelites made their booths, they then would dress in their finest clothes usually white and then dwell in these booths. Notice how this is similar to when the martyred saints are given white robes to wear. The Jews during the feast lived in temporary shelters for seven days following the harvest. This so clearly parallels the rapture harvest of the church and how there will be many converts after the main harvest. The martyrs in Revelation have to wait the seven years for their brethren to all be martyred because they missed the rapture!

They have not been resurrected as yet, and they have to wait under the altar. They cry, "How long, O Lord, holy and true, dost thou not judge and avenge our blood on them that dwell on the earth?" (Revelation 6:10). This is not the normal response of a Christian; that's because these martyrs are not the church, but they do have a part in the first resurrection (Revelation 20:4–6). Example: when Stephen was martyred, he said, "Lord, lay not this sin to their charge." And when he had said this, he fell asleep (Acts 7:60).

This is a completely different response to what the martyrs cry in Revelation 6:10. They cry for vengeance not forgiveness; that's because the time of grace has ended. The Lamb is no longer sitting on the throne of grace (Revelation 5:6–7). The martyrs in the Revelation are the gleanings that follow the main harvest (Leviticus 19:9; 23:22). Grapes would not be picked again following the main harvest, and they were mainly left for the poor and the foreigners. This again shows the tribulation period, and it helps to illustrate the martyrs' place as the gleanings during the Feast of Tabernacles. The first resurrection is not over completely until the gleanings of the poor and foreigners are brought in. Jeremiah 6:9 says, "Those who remain in Israel will be like grapes thoroughly gleaned from a vine. So go over them again, as though you were a grape harvester passing your hand over the branches one last time" (Jeremiah 6:9). This festival is also known as the Feast of Ingatherings (Exodus 23:16).

> After this I beheld, and, lo, a great multitude, which no man could number, of all nations, and kindreds, and people, and tongues, stood before the throne, and before the Lamb, clothed with white robes, and palms in their hands; And cried with a loud voice, saying, Salvation to our God which sitteth upon throne, and unto the Lamb.
>
> Revelation 7:9

> And one of the elders answered, saying unto me, What are these which are arrayed in white robes? And whence came they? And I said unto him, Sir, thou knowest. And he said to me, These are they which came out of great tribulation, and have washed their robes, and made them white in the blood of the Lamb.
>
> Revelation 7:13–14

They were given palm branches, and like the Jews who still wait for Messiah, they wave their palm branches looking ahead in the future. The similarities are unmistakable, the Jews wait in booths or temporary shelters for seven days dressed in white, waving palm branches and looking for Messiah, and the martyred saints in white robes wave their palm branches and wait under the altar seven years waiting to be resurrected. Both groups are waiting for the Lord. The church was raptured seven years ago, but both these groups and events flow together after the harvest and are pictured within the week of Feast of Tabernacles.

Harvest of Man

Daniel's seventieth week = seven years,
starts after the rapture harvest.
One week of Feast of Tabernacles, now =
seven years, for the harvest of man.
The Jews
They dress in white
They wave palm branches
They look ahead for Messiah to come
Jesus said, you will not see me until you say, Blessed
is he who comes in the name of the Lord.
The martyrs do the same things
They are also dressed in white
They have palm branches in their hands
They call for vengeance not grace (because
grace ended at the rapture)
They look ahead to be resurrected
Hallel Psalms include the martyrs of Revelation
Precious in the sight of the Lord is the
death of his saints (Psalm 116:15)
Seventy weeks determined upon the Jews
Seventy bulls are sacrificed for the Gentiles
The martyrs are the gleanings of the har-
vest brought in at the end of the week.
Both the Jews and the Gentiles dealt with in
Revelation during the harvest of man.
The church is missing because she precedes the feast.
Mid-trib or post-trib views are not seen
within the Feast of Tabernacles.
Only the pre-trib view is demonstrated within the feast.

The simple fact that the martyrs in Revelation have white robes and are called saints does not mean that they are the church especially in light of the harvest and the Feast of Tabernacles. Moreover the martyred saints have palm branches in their hands just like the Jews used during the time of the feast that (followed the harvest.) The twenty-four elders are different. They picture the Old and

New Testament saints who were redeemed by the blood of the Lamb back in Revelation four and five. They have thrones to sit on and have crowns on their heads, and they throw them before the throne. They don't have palm branches in their hands which is a point worth the making. But these martyred saints are waiting under the altar with palm branches, and this is an accurate picture of the Feast of Tabernacles with the palm branches being used, as they are looking ahead, waiting to be resurrected as the Jews look ahead for Messiah to come.

These palm branches were called a lulav. They are made from branches of palms, myrtles, and willows and then tied together. The lulavs, or palm branches, were used by the people to wave during the temple service. The Jews would come to the temple holding an etrog, or citrus fruit. This was symbolic of the fruit of the promised land, and the booths are temporary shelters. They are all symbols of the Feast of Tabernacles as they wait for Messiah. It is this typology that helps us understand who the martyrs are in the book of Revelation, because once you see it you'll see the harvest picture of man in Revelation, as it is shown in the Feast of Tabernacles.

There were two noteworthy features that were found in the temple service of the Feast of Tabernacles. One was the pouring of water in the temple; it lasted six days climaxing on the seventh day. That day is called, Hoshanna Rabbah, the Day of Great Hosanna! Hoshanna Rabbah had great Messianic significance. This was the pouring of the water from the golden pitcher. It took place as the custom was with the blasting of trumpets by the priests and the singing of the Hallel Psalms 113–118. They would wave their Lulavs or palm branches. They shouted, "Save Now, I beseech thee, O LORD: O LORD, I beseech thee, send now prosperity. Blessed is he that cometh in the name of the Lord" (Psalm 118:25–26).

The next feature within the temple service was the illumination of the temple. They used four great towering candlesticks with four golden bowls upon them. The priests would climb up and fill these bowls with ten gallons of oil each. This along with the pilgrims who came with torches and lamps made for a breathtaking sight under the dark blue light of night. Jerusalem was illuminated throughout with glowing light during this ceremony. There are all kinds of great symbolism found here in the Feast of Tabernacles.

When Jesus came into Jerusalem as the story is told, the people wanted to proclaim him king right then and there, but his time had not yet come. They waved the palm branches and shouted Hosanna to the Son of David! During the last day of the great Feast of Tabernacles, "Jesus stood and cried, saying, If any man thirst, let him come unto me, and drink. He that believeth on me, as the Scripture hath said, out of his belly shall flow rivers of living water" (John 7:37–38). At or near the end of the feast, Jesus said, "I am the light of the world: he that followeth me shall not walk in darkness, but shall have the light of life" (John 8:12). This is a marvelous account of the people instinctively knowing who Jesus was and then getting palm branches and shouting, "Hosanna: Blessed is the King of Israel that cometh in the name of the Lord" (John 12:12–13). There is a prophetic picture in Matthew 21:6–16, where they throw branches down in front of Jesus saying Hosanna to the Son of David!

> And when the chief priests and scribes saw the wonderful things that he did, and the children crying in the temple, and saying, Hosanna to the son of David; they were sore displeased, And said unto him, Hearest thou what these say? And Jesus saith unto them, Yea; have ye never read, Out of the mouths of babes and sucklings thou hast perfected praise?
>
> Matthew 21:15–16

This is why the Feast of Tabernacles speaks to the ear of faith and is such a prophetic feast. It is the only major feast that is yet to be fulfilled. This is why the harvest at the end of the age shall shadow these events that are pictured in the Feast of Tabernacles. The martyred saints are clearly within this picture as they wait to be resurrected; they are the gleanings of the first resurrection (Revelation 20:4–6). Remember there was a main harvest before the one week could begin, the beautiful harvest of his church. But to the Jews Jesus said, "Ye shall not see me henceforth, till ye shall say, Blessed is he that cometh in the name of the Lord" (Matthew 23:39).

Oh, that we would have an awareness of the things that differ
that truly do make a difference
From the Son of man to the Son of God
two titles we see,
but what is the difference as we read?
Many go down the wrong road to conclude
things never intended they should include.
For far better to first hear his voice
than to see him from earth, and have no choice
In the clouds as they see from the earth
It's the Son of man coming; it's Messiah they see.
But if you're with the Son of God,
you'll appear in the heavens as Messiah they see
Because you know him, his title you see
You return with him
and there in the clouds you'll be

The Son of man

The title Son of man is misunderstood by many in Matthew 24. It can be corrected if one looks at it up against the title Son of God in the same book of Matthew. This chapter goes along with the elect chapter and further helps lace together and demonstrate that the coming of the Son of man will be witnessed by the Jews and those left on earth. It is very clear that only believers and demons recognized Jesus throughout the Gospel of Matthew as Son of God, not the Son of man. The Son of man was in reference to the Jewish nation. This is a big problem for those trying to stick the church into being the elect in Matthew 24. The church sees Jesus as the Son of God. This is a glaring problem for all pre-wrath and post-trib people. All they have to do is look through Matthew and compare those Scriptures, and they'll see that they have missed this point; and it is not accurate to try to cram the church into seeing the Son of man when we can demonstrate the opposite. As believers, the church will hear the voice of the Son of God, and we will see the Son of God (John 5:25). It has become an obvious mistake, but people do keep repeating this error of saying the church will be on earth and see the Son of man. I had one pre-wrath person say to me, "it should just say it plainly." The fact of the matter is it does plainly say it; it's just that people have misapplied the two different terms.

When discussing the elect and the coming of the Son of man, as seen in Matthew 24 and Mark 13, we see that many people have misunderstood this terminology found in these books. There is much confusion today because people are trying so hard to see the church in every verse in the four gospels. The truth is the church as having Gentiles in it did not exist until the book of Acts. The disciples at that time were not under the new covenant yet. Jesus hadn't died yet, nor was the veil rent in two. People try so hard at times to make everything in the gospels conform to what they think it should say about the church, and that can be misleading.

The term Son of man is one that focuses on Jesus' coming as a man and offering the kingdom of heaven to the Jews, which they rejected. The book of Matthew starts off by mentioning the Davidic Covenant, which is one of kingship, and then the Abrahamic Covenant, which is one of promise, and now God is about to do a new thing through Jesus (2 Samuel 7:8–16 and Genesis 15:18). The whole book of Matthew when referring to the Son of man is Jesus making himself known to the Jews and the fact that he would have to suffer and be put to death as the Son of man. The book of Matthew was the tying up of the old promises to the fathers (Romans 15:8). Jesus said, "I am not sent but to the lost sheep of the house of Israel" (Matthew 15:24).

In the book of Matthew, the phrase is not seen as having any reference to the church at all. It is all about Jesus coming as a man and offering the kingdom of heaven to the Jews. It will be the Jews and the Gentiles that see Jesus coming as the Son of man, and it reflects the coming kingdom of heaven on earth for the Jews. All the way through Matthew, it reveals an earthly mission of Jesus when using that phrase. It is about things such as the Son of man is Lord of the Sabbath, which is Jewish. He also said, "Behold, we go up to Jerusalem; and the Son of man shall be betrayed unto the chief priests and unto the scribes, and they shall condemn him to death" (Matthew 20:18). Over and over again throughout the book of Matthew, Jesus states what his mission is to the Jews and his coming death. Jesus even uses typology about his own death: "Jonas was three days and three nights in the whale's belly; so shall the Son of man be three days and three nights in the heart of the earth" (Matthew 12:40). The Son of man soweth good seed and, "The field is the world." This again points out the earthly intention and meaning for the Son of man.

Even when the angels are sent forth to reap the earth, it is still seen in an earthly setting. The Son of man shall be betrayed and killed on earth (Matthew 17:22–23). Jesus died as a perfect man, the Lamb of God, and the book of Matthew is very clear about the intentions of his coming as the Son of man. Even at the judgment of the nations as seen in Matthew 19:28, we see that it is still the Son of man that will sit on the throne, on earth. Jesus tells of his death as he must go to Jerusalem to be betrayed and condemned to death, again all earthly scenes.

Then the confusion by so many people in Matthew chapter twenty-four in regards to the apocalypse. You have the term the Son of man, and then you also have all the Jewish distinctions made on top of that. Those Jews that are in Judea are to flee to the mountains, and they are to pray that their flight be not in winter or on the Sabbath. How much more Jewish can it get? The sun will be darkened, thereby excluding all Christians because we are of the light, and children of the day; we don't fit in Matthew 24 at all. Out of twenty-eight verses in Matthew that use the phrase Son of man, they all point to an earthly, Jewish, sacrificial perspective. That term does not reveal the full majesty of who Christ is because Jesus had to offer the earthly kingdom of heaven to the Jews first as seen in Matthew 10:1–8. That is why Jesus told his disciples to not go unto the Gentiles because he was offering the kingdom of heaven on earth to the Jews first. It will be the Jews who see Jesus coming as the Son of man in Matthew 24.

Son of God

At the first resurrection, which is still future and includes the church, the dead in Christ will hear the voice of the Son of God, not the Son of man (John 5:25). The Son of man is for the Jews in reference to the earth. Now when we look at the same book of Matthew and look at the term Son of God, all the previous statements are confirmed. Moreover, if you do a study of the gospel of Matthew and compare both terms side by side, you will see that the term Son of God has a far more revealing title and authority given to it, and it is not restricted to time and place and the Jews, as it is with the term Son of man.

When the term Son of God is used in the book of Matthew, the first three are proclaimed by Satan and his demons. This is because they are spirit beings, and they see his eternal position. "And when the tempter came to him, he said, If thou be the Son of God, command that these stones be made bread" (Matthew 4:3).

This was Satan who said this. He knows who Jesus is, and that's why in Matthew 4:6 Satan again says, "If thou be the Son of God, cast thyself down." Satan is tempting the Son of God, and that title reveals more about Jesus, his Majesty and authority, and that is a much larger role as that of the Son of man, as it only concerns the Jews and his earthly mission.

The demons also recognize Jesus in his full role as the Son of God, because it transcends beyond just the earthly. "And, behold they cried out, saying, What have we to do with thee, Jesus, thou Son of God? Art thou come hither to torment us before the time?" (Matthew 8:28–29). It is clear that Satan and his angels weren't confused about who he was; they knew he was the Son of God! They didn't bother with the term Son of man.

Then the glorious account of Jesus walking on the water. "And when the disciples saw him walking on the sea, they were troubled, saying, It is a spirit; and they cried out for fear" (Matthew 14:26). Jesus speaks to them, and then Peter asked Jesus if he can come to him on the water. "And he said, Come. And when Peter was come down out of the ship, he walked on the water, to go to Jesus"

(Matthew 14:29). The disciples saw all this and how the sea went calm as they came into the ship. "Then they that were in the ship came and worshipped him, saying, Of a truth thou art the Son of God" (Matthew 14:32–33). So here we have the disciples seeing Jesus beyond his Son of man role, and they recognize him and worship him as, the Son of God. So it is believers and those who worship Jesus that recognize him as the Son of God.

Now we get to the next two accounts that use both terms in Matthew. They illustrate the earthly mission as the Lamb that would be slain, and his Lordship over all things. Jesus asked his disciples,

> Whom do men say that I the Son of man am? And they said, Some say that thou art John the Baptist: some, Elias; and others, Jeremias, or one of the prophets. He saith unto them, But whom say ye that I am? And Simon Peter answered and said, Thou art the Christ, the Son of God. And Jesus answered and said unto him, Blessed art thou, Simon Barjona: for flesh and blood hath not revealed it unto thee, but my Father which is in heaven.
>
> Matthew 16:13–17

The disciples saw him beyond his earthly mission, which they didn't fully understand at the time. In these verses, Jesus declares that he is the Son of man, but the disciples still see him as the Son of God! Laid out in front of us here is the earthly and the heavenly aspects of Jesus.

Then the account in Matthew 26:62–64 defines it even further.

> And the high priest answered and said unto him, I adjure thee by the living God, that thou tell us whether thou be the Christ, the Son of God. Jesus saith unto him, Thou hast said: nevertheless I say unto you, Hereafter shall ye see the Son of man sitting on the right hand of power, and coming in the clouds of heaven.
>
> Matthew 26:62–64

We see Jesus lets the high priest say it, and then Jesus confirms it; but then Jesus goes right back to referring to himself as the Son of man. Here again in the gospel of Matthew, we see both roles presented to us, his earthly mission as Son of man and his royal heavenly title as Son of God. Spirit beings understood who he was, and his followers worshiped him as Son of God. Even those that crucified Jesus "saw the earthquake, and those things that were done, they feared greatly, saying, Truly this was the Son of God" (Matthew 27:54).

When we see the gospel of Matthew with these titles and terms properly understood, it helps to clear up much of the confusion about Jesus' role as Son of man and the larger role he has as the Son of God. It is very evident that there are lots of people that have either missed this or ignored what is meant by the coming of the Son of man in Matthew 24. There are large groups of Christians that seem to be determined to replace Israel with the church in Matthew 24, but once you see how the Son of God is used in contrast to the Son of man in the same book, you have a better understanding of the intent of the gospels. This actually helps to establish who the elect are in Matthew 24. It will be the Jews who are the elect on the earth at that time, and it is the Jews and Gentiles that are left on earth that will see Jesus coming in the clouds as the Son of man. If the church was still on earth, we would see him coming as the Son of God!

For further affirmation, see 1 John chapters four and five. John the beloved calls the church the beloved all throughout, and he refers to all who put their faith in Jesus, the Son of God, as having eternal life (1 John 5:10–13, Acts 8:37). This underscores the fact that those elect in Matthew 24 are not Christians but Jews. "And we know that the Son of God is come, and hath given us an understanding, that we may know him that is true, and we are in him that is true, even in his Son Jesus Christ. This is the true God, and eternal life" (1 John 5:20). The church is not going to be on earth at the end of the age as though we had no clue as to what is happening. "Even the mystery which hath been hid from the ages and from generations, but now is made manifest to his saints: To whom God would make known what is the riches of the glory of this mystery among the Gentiles; which is Christ in you, the hope of glory" (Colossians 1:26–27). With all these scriptural facts about the church seeing Jesus as the Son of God, does anyone truly want to contradict that by saying we will be there on earth the last day and we will see him as the Son of man?

The Blind Man

I love the story of the blind man from birth receiving his sight in John 9:1–38. The Pharisees were troubled by his healing on the Sabbath so they interrogated the man and then finally cast him out.

> Jesus heard that they had cast him out; and when he had found him, he said unto him, Dost thou believe on the Son of God? He answered and said, who is he, Lord, that I might believe on him? And Jesus said unto him, Thou hast both seen him, and it is he that talketh with thee. And he said, Lord, I believe. And he worshipped him.
>
> John 9:35–38

The love of Jesus is revealed here in that Jesus sought him out because he had healed him and the Jews threw him out of the temple for it. The man had never seen Jesus, so when Jesus finds the man, he gives him a direct chance to believe on him as the Son of God. Jesus didn't say anything about the Son of man, here again showing that the followers of Jesus will see him as the Son of God.

Then the accounts of mocking by the people.

> And they that passed by reviled him, wagging their heads, And saying, Thou that destroyest the temple, and buildest it in three days, save thyself. If thou be the Son of God, come down from the cross. Likewise also the chief priests mocking him, with the scribes and elders, said, He saved others; himself he cannot save. If he be the King of Israel, let him now come down from the cross, and we will believe him. He trusted in God; let him deliver him now, if he will have him: for he said, I am the Son of God.
>
> Matthew 27:39–43

They used the term Son of God, but they mocked him. All of this calls attention to the fact that the Jews refused to see Jesus as the Son of God. Only a small group of believers and Satan and his demons recognized Jesus as the Son of God.

Then one last interesting account to ponder.

> And, behold, the veil of the temple was rent in twain from the top to the bottom; and the earth did quake, and the rocks rent; And the graves were opened; and many bodies of the saints which slept arose, And came out of the graves after his resurrection, and went into the holy city, and appeared unto many. Now when the centurion, and they that were with him, watching Jesus, saw the earthquake, and those things that were done, they feared greatly, saying, Truly this was the Son of God.
>
> Matthew 27:51–54

It is an interesting point that this was not said by the Jews. It was said by the centurion and those with him, and those would have been Roman guards. This lends itself to the guards and the centurion believing on Jesus as the Son of God. The other possibility would be that they knew he was the Son of God, just as the demons knew it, but they did not worship him. In Mark 15:39 it says that the centurion said, "Truly this man was the Son of God." It appears that he became a believer because Jesus said, "for flesh and blood hath not revealed it unto thee, but my Father which is in heaven" (Matthew 16:17).

Let us not forget that to the church Jesus is the Son of God; that is clear. To the Jews he is the Son of man. We only encourage error if we undervalue the importance of Jesus' title as the Son of God. We have been enlightened to understand the mystery in Christ. We won't be on the earth looking to heaven and saying something silly like, "Look, there's someone like the Son of man coming in the clouds!" That would indicate that we didn't know him as the Son of God. "But these are written, that ye might believe that Jesus is the Christ, the Son of God; and that believing ye might have life through his name"

(John 20:31). Appearing in glory and returning in the clouds, we shall appear with Jesus our Lord and Savior, the Son of God. Colossians 3:4. People left on earth will see the Son of man coming with the armies of heaven.

As the elect are understood,
the haze of replacement theology blows away,
Revealing a mountain of Scripture in its stay.
With a blast from the great trumpet,
the mighty angels will go
All across the world
to bring sons and daughters home.

The Elect

Who are the Elect on Earth When the Lord Returns? Mark 13:27 and Matthew 24:31

This chapter deals with the classic misapplied explanation of what Jesus said in the above Scriptures concerning the elect. If you can explain these two Scriptures in their proper setting, then the whole argument for these elect being the church at that time just goes away. As the Son of man chapter points out, these elect cannot be Christians. There are no other supporting Scriptures to back up any real argument for the church being the elect on earth at that time other than these two verses that are many times misapplied. Why are there no other Scriptures to support such a claim? Why are there so many phrases that point to the Jews? Why do so many Christians get this wrong in the clear light of all the Jewish references? Seemingly without realizing it, some Christians have embraced replacement theology.

One thing you'll find out right away when talking with people who seem determined to put the church into Matthew 24 and Mark 13, they don't seem to recollect much about the Old Testament, because if they did they would see how easily the Jews fit into these verses. The Old Testament is not even considered when they are talking about these things, it would certainly disprove what they are saying. It really is remarkable to see how large a portion of Scripture deals with this from the Old Testament as it concerns the Jews.

The Bible is spilling over with terms like gathered, scattered, from the uttermost parts of the earth, in the dark and cloudy day, and those in Judea fleeing into the mountains praying it's not on the Sabbath. The beauties of truth are; there are far too many

Jewish references and Jewish phrases being used here. If you're not careful, you'll end up arguing against a mountain of Scripture if you embrace replacement theology. I posted about this topic on a Web site of pre-wrath and post-trib people, and none of them could explain away with any biblical backing what I was pointing out to them.

There are many believers who read these Scriptures, and they will make the assumption that these elect are the church. Whether they know it or not, they have embraced the replacement-theology view of Scripture. This view tries to redefine and disregards Old Testament Scriptures, and what the Bible says so definitively about things like the elect and the Jews inheriting the land forever. But as we will see, there are key words and phrases that can only apply to Israel. Really, we are talking about the same reference concerning the elect at the end of the age because these references are one in the same; they just happen to be in Matthew 24 and Mark 13. It's the same Olivet discourse as it concerns the elect. The account is found in both books because each book has a different nuance or angle that it reveals.

So then we really have one reference for the elect at the end of the age in the gospels, when the Son of man sends forth his angels to gather them. Who are they? If you're a pre-wrath or post-trib believer, it will be promoted with that angle, and if you're a pre-trib believer, you'll just realize that there are a lot of people trying really hard to place the church into this scenario to take Israel's place, all the while neglecting the multitude of Scriptures from the Old Testament that have come down to us that declare otherwise.

Some people will insist that these elect are the church while not even considering Israel's place in Scripture. They say they believe the church will go through the tribulation to be purified, forgetting all the Scriptures handed down from the long ages. They make two big mistakes right from the start. The one is if the blood of Christ cannot purify the church, nothing can. The other being that those who really believe that the church will go through the tribulation are forced to admit that they are not looking for Jesus now. Both of these ideas are in error, and it makes you wonder why some Christians would be fooled into thinking these things.

"And then he shall send His angels, and shall gather together

His elect from the four winds, from the uttermost part of the earth to the uttermost part of heaven" (Mark 13:27).

Matthew 24:31 says, "And He shall send His angels with a great sound of a trumpet, and they shall gather together his elect from the four winds, from one end of heaven to the other."

Understand the word election—it simply means to be picked out. A Young's or Strong's concordance will show that elect means chosen. The word election designates a sovereign or divine purpose. Some people want to think that the word elect is always referring to the church. But, if you search this out throughout the Bible, you will see that the church, Israel, and even angels are referred to as the elect.

There are a lot of false ideas and teachings around because people make this assumption about the church being the only group of elect found in the Bible. It almost makes you want to look at these people who say this and ask them, "Do you think Israel still exists?" They will look like a deer in the headlights because you have just spotlighted them and now they have to give a biblical reason as to why Israel no longer exists. They have to try to tell you how the Old Testament is no longer valid as it concerns the Jews. Of course, this is ridiculous, but that is the only direction they can go if they cling to the view of the church being the only elect in the Bible. We need to give way to the Scriptures and the divine providence of God in these matters; then the light of truth will shine out the clearer.

Israel
Chosen and Elect

"For the Lord hath chosen Jacob unto himself, and Israel for his peculiar treasure" (Psalm 135:4, 12). "Blessed is the nation whose God is the Lord; and the people whom he hath chosen for his own inheritance" (Psalm 33:12). Scripture tells us that Israel is a chosen nation (Isaiah 41:8–9; 44:1). Now the question is, are they also called the elect? And much to the dismay of those who would only look at the church as being the elect in the Bible, surprise, Israel is directly called the elect (Isaiah 45:4; 65:9; 65:22). Even in the New Testament, Israel is referred to as the elect. "As concerning the gospel, they are enemies for your sakes: but as touching the election, they are beloved for the father's sakes" (Romans 11:25, 28). The church is also called the elect (Romans 8:33, Colossians 3:12, 1 Thessalonians 1:4, 1 Peter 5:13).

Throughout the holy Scriptures, Israel is referred to as the elect in the Old Testament and in the New Testament. The church has become the elect, because of the blindness of Israel for not recognizing their Messiah (Romans 11:22, 25, 28). After the rapture of the church, Israel once again becomes the elect for the setting up of her promised; kingdom of heaven on earth. To better understand this, you must look at the promises God has for the church and the promises God has for Israel. They are entirely different promises, so we need to respect what is said about each group and try not to redefine or replace what is already revealed in Scripture. We need to stay away from replacement theology, which says that the church somehow replaced Israel.

Israel's Promises

The promises for Israel are earthly; they will have their kingdom upon the earth. This purpose is shown in Deuteronomy 7:6, where the Lord hath chosen Israel. "The LORD thy God hath chosen thee to be a special people unto himself, above all people that are upon the face of the earth." They will have one shepherd. It is then that the King, Jesus, will sit upon the throne of David (Luke 1:32–33). The Jews will inherit the land forever (Genesis 13:15; Ezekiel 37:24–25; 34:11–16, 23–25; Isaiah 40:9–11; 60:20–21; Daniel 2:44; Jeremiah 23:5–6; 32:37–40; 2 Samuel 7:12–16; Hosea 3:4–5; John 10:16). After reading these infallible statements from Scripture, one is forced to take into account that Israel will indeed inherit the land forever and will have her messianic earthly kingdom, in their land and upon the earth. It is unseemly to see how many Christians have (ignored) all these Scriptures that shed so much light about who the elect are. It seems that everyone is trying to steal Israel's land and promises these days, but this is why it is called the promised land. This promise is for the Jews, not the church or anyone else.

In this age of the church, God is calling out to Jews and Gentiles (Romans 10:1, 19).

> Simeon hath declared how God at the first did visit the Gentiles, to take out of them a people for his name. And to this agree the words of the Prophets; as it is written, After this I will return, and will build again the Tabernacle of David, which is fallen down and will build again the ruins thereof, and I will set it up.
>
> Acts 15:14–16

You see it is after this—or after the church has been raptured out of this world—that God will then return and set up the kingdom on earth. This is why the church is seen in mystery due to the blindness of Israel, but the Lord will still use the Jews after the church in mystery is gone from the earth.

After the church is raptured, God will deal with Israel again, and they shall be sifted as corn (Amos 9:9–11; Ezekiel 20:37–38). This is the purging Israel will receive after the church age (Zechariah 13:6–9, Malachi 3:2–4). The church in mystery is gone, and God is again dealing with Israel during the tribulation. "Alas! For that day is great, so that none is like it: it is even the time of Jacob's trouble; but he shall be saved out of it" (Jeremiah 30:7–9).

> For the LORD hath called thee as a woman forsaken and grieved in spirit, and a wife of youth, when thou wast refused, saith thy God. For a small moment have I forsaken thee, but with great mercies will I gather thee. In a little wrath I hid my face from thee for a moment; but with everlasting kindness will I have mercy on thee, saith the Lord thy Redeemer.
>
> Isaiah 54:6–8

The small moment spoken of here is the seven-year tribulation period.

God will not sift Israel until he has taken out from among the Gentiles a people for his name, (the church). After all, this singly fits with the promises for the church. The promises for the church are heavenly. Israel is not the church, and the church is not Israel. The two have different promises, and if people don't see this, they won't understand last day things in the Bible. This needs to be stated again. If you don't see that the church and Israel have different promises, you're probably reading the Bible trying to replace Israel, disregarding the clear distinctions that are made between both in Scripture. The plainest fact becomes a blur if you can't see these differences. You have no starting point to understand, and God is not the author of confusion.

If God says the land is for Israel, and then you or I come along and say it's for someone else, it is a most grievous error to make. To directly contradict the Word of the Lord is dangerous. When the Lord says he gave the land to Israel forever, we need to believe his word and try not to redefine what is so clearly stated. We do well to remember that he intended this land for Israel, forever. "For we can do nothing against the truth, but for the truth" (2 Corinthians 13:7–8).

The Church Will Sit in Heavenly Places

We should also respect the fact that Jesus told his church that we are not of this world. Our Lord and Savior Jesus has gone to prepare a place for the church in heaven (John 14:2–3). The church is not of this world. Jesus said, "If you were of the world, the world would love its own: but because ye are not of the world, but I have chosen ye out of the world, therefore the world hateth you" (John 15:19). The promises for the church are in heaven. Our inheritance is reserved in heaven (1 Peter 1:4). Our hope is laid up in heaven (Colossians 1:5). Our treasure is in heaven (Matthew 6:20, Luke 12:33). The church will be joint heirs with Christ (Romans 8:17, Galatians 4:7). We shall also reign with him over this kingdom (Luke 22:29). The church shall be made kings and priests (Revelation 1:6; 5:10). The grand fact is there are many more Scriptures that verify our place in heaven with Christ. This all stands in stark contrast to the Jews and their earthly kingdom.

One of the most sparkling reasons the church is not the elect then on earth is the fact that the church returns with Jesus. The church being his bride will return in total victory with the armies of heaven. It will be seen that the church will have a glorious victory over our enemies and the enemies of Christ (Zechariah 14:5).

The Lord will come with all his saints (1 Thessalonians 3:13; 4:14; Jude 14; Deuteronomy 33:2; Revelation 19:7–14). Many people even within the church do not consider this because they have made the mistake of thinking that the elect in Matthew 24 and Mark 13 can only be the church. How sad, and it shows how little some know of the Old Testament Scriptures that squarely point to the Jews in this time period. Consider the matter, to have this kind of misunderstanding, you have to disregard the entire Old Testament concerning Israel and her role in the last seven years.

Some will only look at the word elect in Matthew and Mark and then automatically assume it's the church without ever reading the vast number of Old Testament Scriptures. At the Second Coming when the scroll of the sky is rolled away, the church will ride down from glory upon white horses in total victory. She won't be left on earth to be bloodied and martyred. Upon the day chosen, as the Lord returns, he will be accompanied by a cloud of horsemen riding upon the train of his glory!

The Harvest

The lament of Jesus over Jerusalem.

> O Jerusalem, Jerusalem, thou that killest the prophets, and stonest them which are sent unto thee, how often would I have gathered thy children together, even as a hen gathereth her chickens under her wings, and ye would not. Behold your house is left unto you desolate. For I say unto you, Ye shall not see me henceforth, till ye shall say, Blessed is he that cometh in the name of the Lord.
>
> Matthew 23:37–39

Jesus said this before the Olivet discourse where he mentions the tribulation upon the Holy City and the Jews. Jesus was prophesying that the Jews would call upon the name of the Lord at the end of the age harvest, as they do during the end of the week-long harvest period of the Feast of Tabernacles.

The harvest is the end of the age, and the reapers are the

angels (Matthew 13:39). When Jesus comes for the church, he will come for it himself and will present it unto himself (John 14:2–3, 1 Thessalonians 4:14–18, Ephesians 5:27, 32). The church won't be gathered by angels as the Jewish elect are in Matthew 24 and Mark 13. In the four gospels, Jesus was talking to the Jews and his Jewish disciples. He was not talking to his church about fleeing from Judea into the mountains and praying that their flight be not on the Sabbath. The church won't be brought before the synagogues in those days because that was spoken directly to the Jews.

How is it that the church is now in Jerusalem at this time of the end, praying that our flight be not on the Sabbath? Did the church all of a sudden turn into orthodox Jews? Of course not, and this is a glaring mistake for people who think the elect at this time are the church. Let them explain how it is that we are in Israel praying that our flight be not on the Sabbath. This doesn't apply to the church at all, and using that kind of logic you could say when Israel is called the elect in the Old Testament, it must be talking about the church as though Israel doesn't exist anymore and all of a sudden the church has somehow mysteriously taken Israel's place. The ugly head of replacement theology is seen here when people do this, and we cannot let people just redefine the Scriptures to suit their preferred genre.

This type of thinking is not scriptural, and yet this is the type of logic that people are using today to say the church is the elect at the coming of the Son of man in Matthew 24 and Mark 13. Replacement theology is a faulty belief that says the church is spiritual Israel and has taken over all of the promises for Israel. First of all the Lord changes not, and when he says he will not give the land to another people, it is a very dangerous thing to directly contradict such a clear declaration. It should also concern us that this type of circular reasoning stirs up resentment against the Jews, that somehow she really doesn't exist anymore, and none us should stand for that. If we're not careful, we'll find ourselves siding with the Palestinians against Israel. We need to recognize that Israel is blind right now, but the Lord is not through with the nation of Israel (Romans 11:1–8). We are commanded to pray for the peace of Jerusalem, and that should show us the Lord's concern for her.

These warnings were given to the Jewish nation in Matthew

24:31 and Mark 13:27 about what would happen in the tribulation and right at the end of the age, as it concerns the Jews and those Gentiles still alive on earth. Remember when Jesus said this there wasn't a church born yet, and it's hard to even find a Gentile in the Scriptures that heard what Jesus said. Jesus' disciples at that time were still under the old covenant, and the veil was not yet torn in two. Some people will stubbornly refuse to see that Israel is God's elect after the rapture. But when the church is raptured into glory, Israel becomes the elect again on earth. The Lord then turns to deal with Israel at the end of the age to complete Daniel's seventieth week that was determined upon the Jews and the Holy City of Jerusalem (Daniel 7:18; 9:24; Acts 15:13–16).

In the harvest scene at the end of the age, there is no mention of angels gathering the church. Our Lord Jesus will come personally for the church himself, in a moment, in the twinkling of an eye seven years prior. Once the Lord has taken out his church from off the earth, it's then we see between these two extremes, the emphasis goes right back on Israel.

> And it shall come to pass in that day, that the LORD shall beat off from the channel of the river unto the stream of Egypt, and ye shall be gathered one by one, O ye children of Israel. And it shall come to pass in that day, that the great trumpet shall be blown, and they shall come which were ready to perish in the land of Assyria, and the outcasts in the land of Egypt, and shall worship the LORD in the holy mount at Jerusalem.
>
> Isaiah 27:12–13

This points out with great authority that Israel will be gathered one by one in that day. The great trumpet shall be blown; then they shall worship the Lord in the holy mount at Jerusalem. It is really amazing to think that so many people who are pre-wrath or post-trib have missed this completely. They have not considered that the great trumpet here is the same great trumpet in Matthew 24:31 (Zechariah 9:14–17, Zephaniah 1:15–16). "All ye inhabitants of the world, and dwellers on the earth, see ye, when he lifteth up the ensign on the mountains; and when he bloweth a trumpet, hear ye" (Isaiah 18:3).

This is the scene at the end of the age harvest, and it is clearly united to the gathering of Israel. It is the same event, and it concerns the Jews not the church. Here we have the great trumpet being blown in the Old Testament concerning the Jews being brought back to their land. Why is it that people have not considered these Scriptures when talking about the elect? Mind you, they are clearly for Israel and in no way apply to the church.

More and more testimony that Israel is gathered by angels and will be fetched back to their land: "If any of thine be driven out unto the outmost parts of heaven, from thence will the LORD thy God gather thee, and from thence will he fetch thee" (Deuteronomy 30:3–6). Wilson Old Testament Word Studies says the word fetch means "To take away, to remove, To take up, to fetch home again." This task will be given to the holy angels to carry out, when the end of the harvest comes. These are not Jews returning to their land only, because in verse six you see that in that day the Lord will circumcise their hearts to love the Lord their God. This will not happen until the LORD comes back, and they look upon him whom they have pierced (Zechariah 12:10; Jeremiah 32:37–40).

A Fire Shall Devour before Him

Then the awesome apocalyptic picture of judgment.

> Our God shall come, and shall not keep silence: A fire shall devour before him, and it shall be very tempestuous round about him. He shall call to the heaven from above, and to the earth, that he may judge his people. Gather my saints together unto me; those that have made a covenant with me by sacrifice.
>
> Psalm 50:3–7

Verse seven identifies who is being gathered. "Hear, O my people; and I will speak; O Israel, and I will testify against thee: I am God, even thy God." A couple of things stand out brightly here in these apocalyptic statements. Firstly, this is prophetic of the time our God shall come. Secondly is the fact that he shall call to the heaven from above and to the earth. This is what will happen when the angels are commanded and sent out to gather the elect from the four corners of the earth (Mark 13:27). So, it's the angels that will gather the elect of Israel from the four corners of the earth.

People who dwell on putting the church in Matthew and Mark cannot explain how these verses don't apply to Israel as the elect at the twilight of this age. We see so distinctly impressed on it, that this is referring to Israel. Read verses five and seven of Psalm 50. The timing is the end, and the command is given to gather Israel; and this is what Matthew 24 and Mark 13 are clearly showing. "Bring my sons from far, and my daughters from the ends of the earth" (Isaiah 43:5–6). These are the elect, and it is a most fearsome picture during this time of judgment. "A fire shall devour before him" (Psalm 50:3). Furthermore, and with certainty we see how Israel will be purified by fire:

> But who may abide the day of his coming? And who shall stand when he appeareth? For he is like a refiner's fire, and like a fuller's soap: And he shall sit as a refiner and purifier of silver: and he shall purify the sons of Levi, and purge them as gold and silver, that they may offer unto the LORD an offering in righteousness.
>
> Malachi 3:2–3

The Lord is not coming to purify the church. That's because we are under the blood of Christ, a better covenant. We're not even on the earth for this time of wrath.

With Fury Poured Out

When Israel is gathered, it will be a time of judgment like no other. A time that stands out apart, when fury is poured out.

> As I live, saith the Lord God, surely with a mighty hand, and with a stretched out arm, and with fury poured out, will I rule over you: and I will bring you out from the people, and will gather you out of the countries wherein

> ye are scattered, with a mighty hand, and with a stretched out arm, and with fury poured out.
>
> Ezekiel 20:33–34

The Scripture repeats itself here to get even the critics' attention, and it helps to underscore the colossal magnitude of what is happening on earth as it relates to the Jews. This shows the time of judgment upon the earth: "For in the hand of the LORD is a cup, and the wine is red; it is full of mixture: and he poureth out of the same" (Psalm 75:8). In regards to the wicked, Job 21:20 says, "His eyes shall see his destruction and he shall drink the wrath of the almighty." "Tremble, thou earth, at the presence of the God of Jacob" (Psalm 114:7).

> Therefore thus saith the LORD GOD; Because ye are all become dross, behold, therefore I will gather you into the midst of Jerusalem. As they gather silver, and brass, and iron, and lead, and tin, into the midst of the furnace, to blow the fire upon it, to melt it; so will I gather you in mine anger and in my fury, and I will leave you there, and melt you. Yea, I will gather you, and blow upon you in the fire of my wrath, and ye shall be melted in the midst thereof.
>
> Ezekiel 22:19–22

Does anyone really think this applies to the church? There is no way unless you're embracing replacement theology. We see from the Scriptures how this applies to the harvest timing and the gathering of Israel at the end of the age. It will be a time when fury is poured out from the Almighty. As stated before, the church will return with Jesus. The Jews are the ones gathered in great wrath, not the church (Jeremiah 32:37).

> For behold, the LORD will come with fire, and with his chariots like a whirlwind, to render his anger with fury, and his rebuke with flames of fire. For by fire and by his sword will the LORD plead with all flesh: and the slain of the LORD shall be many.
>
> Isaiah 66:15–16

After that, they (the Jews) are given a new covenant (Jeremiah 32:40). "The LORD shall roar from on high. And the slain of the LORD shall be at that day from one end of the earth even unto the other end of the earth" (Jeremiah 25:30–33).

In the Cloudy and Dark Day

> Behold, the Lord GOD will come with strong hand, and his arm shall rule for him: behold, his reward is with him: and his work before him. He shall feed his flock like a shepherd: he shall gather the lambs with his arm, and carry them in his bosom, and shall gently lead those that are with young.
>
> Isaiah 40:10–11

This is speaking of Jerusalem and those in the cities of Judah. It is pointing out that it is Israel that is gathered in that day. The Lord will gather Israel as a shepherd doth his flock (Jeremiah 31:10). In reference to Israel, Jeremiah 50:6 says, "My people hath been lost sheep." "Israel is a scattered sheep" (Jeremiah 50:17). These references show the elect of Israel being gathered at the end of the age. They also show an awesome scene upon the earth. This is a time of darkness, when the sun shall be darkened and the moon shall not give her light as seen in Matthew 24:29. And then:

> As a shepherd seeketh out his flock in the day that he is among his sheep that are scattered; so will I seek out my sheep, and will deliver them out of all places where they have been scattered in the cloudy and dark day. And I will bring them out from the people, and gather them from the countries, and will bring them to their own land.
>
> Ezekiel 34:12–13

It is hard to argue for the church being on the earth in the cloudy and dark day and then see the whole chapter of Ezekiel 34 talking about Israel and the gathering of Israel, the one shepherd, the throne of David, and the new covenant for the Jews! Let's face it; you can't miss these Scriptures unless you're embracing replacement theology. These Scriptures show a glorious picture of how this all applies to the Jews as the elect at the end of the tribulation, and it's right before the kingdom of heaven is set up. Other references from antiquity include Ezekiel 30:3; Isaiah 13:6–13; Joel 2:1–2, 31–32; 3:12–16; Amos 5:18–20; Zephaniah 1:14–16).

If Israel is a lost sheep and they are gathered in the dark and cloudy day, then it shouldn't be any surprise that they are the elect at the end, at the coming of the Son of man. Moreover, if the sun and moon will not shine and the day of the Lord is darkness, then the elect on earth could not be Christians, because as Christians we are children of the day. We are seen in the realm of light; we are the light of the world (1 Thessalonians 5:5). The church will not be left in the darkness when all light goes out. We will appear with the Lord, at the return of the King! "When Christ, who is our life, shall appear, then shall ye also appear with him in glory" (Colossians 3:4, Isaiah 24:22–23). Notice that this fits in complete harmony with the fact that the church returns with Jesus. We shall appear in the heavens with Christ, the Son of God, and the Jews will see him from the earth as the Son of man (Matthew 24:30–31, Mark 13:26–27).

People who still want to be persecuted in the seven-year tribulation fail to acknowledge the vast amount of Scriptures from the Old Testament that point to this time of unfurled wrath on earth for the Jews. They can't seem to understand that it is the Jews that will be tried in the fire during this time period, a time period that no longer has the grace of God set upon it. Some people will still try to jump into the tribulation ignoring a mountain of Scripture that tells another story. All we can do is try to talk them down from off the ledge using Scripture. It is ironic that some Christians will get so stubborn on this and not believe what the Bible says plainly. The word plainly declares that Israel will go through a time of sifting and purification by trial, in that day. This is never mentioned of the church.

They that are escaped of Israel and he that is left in Jerusalem shall be called holy. And in that day, the Lord will wash away the filth of the daughters of Zion by the spirit of judgment and the spirit of burning (Isaiah 4:2–4). This is all held forth as dealing with Israel. The Scriptures do not mention a time of trouble for the church, and we most certainly haven't replaced Israel. But it does say concerning the Jews, "And I will cause you to pass under the rod, and I will bring you into the bond of the covenant" (Ezekiel 20:37–39). This all focuses on God's elect, Israel, during the tribulation. The church is not even hinted at here because we disappeared in the main harvest that precedes the Feast of Tabernacles. But we see that Israel shall be melted as in a furnace; the Lord will blow upon them in the fire of his wrath (Ezekiel 22:18–22).

"Seventy weeks are determined upon thy people and upon thy holy city, to finish the transgression, and to make reconciliation for iniquity, and to bring in everlasting righteousness, and to anoint the most Holy" (Daniel 9:24). This rebellious world is to be judged, to help set up the millennium kingdom. The church is in heaven getting ready to mount up on white horses. The church will be preparing to rule and reign with Christ! The seventieth week is the last seven years determined upon the Jews and the Holy City.

We see that the Lord will sift the house of Israel as corn is sifted. All the sinners of Israel shall die by the sword (Amos 9:9–11). Israel is refined in the fire, refined as silver is refined, to try them as gold is tried (Zechariah 13:8–9). Two-thirds of the Jews shall be cut off, but one-third will be brought through the fire. And they shall call on his name, and he will hear them; and then the Lord returns (Zechariah 14:1–5).

The unvarnished truth is none of these Old Testament Scriptures apply to the church; they exclusively testify of Israel. When we talk about Matthew 24 and Mark 13 concerning the elect, these Scriptures from the Old Testament point right at the Jews, who are being dealt with as the elect at the close of this age. There are many more Scriptures that flow on and then say that Israel will then be blessed upon the earth. There will be a purging out of the sinners of Israel at that time (before they go into the millennial kingdom as servants). Israel's covenant with death will be disannulled (Isaiah 28:18). The church will not be servants in this kingdom. We will reign with Christ over this kingdom, because we are not of this world (John 17:16). All of this must happen to the Jews and the Holy City of Jerusalem to set up the millennial kingdom upon the earth.

From the Four Corners of the Earth

Mark 13:27

There are still other terms that apply exclusively to Israel. Isaiah 11:10–12 says, "The Lord will recover the remnant of his people," and verse twelve says, "And shall assemble the outcasts of Israel, and gather together the dispersed of Judah from the four corners of the earth." All of Isaiah chapter eleven shows what will happen when the messiah comes. This is a theme that seems to be consistent throughout Scripture concerning Israel. It is found in the term "from the four corners of the earth." Mark 13:27 says, "He shall gather his elect from the four winds, from the uttermost part of the earth to the uttermost part of heaven." References include Isaiah 11:10–12; 43:5–6; Deuteronomy 30:3–6; Nehemiah 1:8–9; Zechariah 2:6–13; Psalm 147:2; Revelation 7:1–8).

The angels go forth to the four corners of the earth at the end of the tribulation. Israel will then be gathered back one by one by the angels at that time (Isaiah 27:12–13). The great trumpet shall be blown. Then they shall worship the Lord in the Holy Mount at Jerusalem. This is what the angels will do when the last day of the harvest comes as seen in Matthew 24 and Mark 13. It is sad to see how some Christians have tried to force the church into this scene while ignoring so much of God's Word.

Jesus prophesied of this time period of the harvest when he said to the Jews. "Ye shall not see me henceforth, till ye shall say, Blessed is he that cometh in the name of the Lord" (Matthew 23:39). What Jesus said was spoken directly to the Jewish nation of Israel; he was not addressing the church at all. The church is not gathered by angels; Jesus will receive us unto himself just as Isaac met Rebekah, alone, in the evening of the day of grace. There is no mention of the church being gathered by angels anywhere in the Bible. People who think the church is gathered by angels should do a study on how Israel is gathered back to Jerusalem, and a different study on how the church is taken by the Lord; they will be startled to see the discrepancy.

The command from God to gather Israel goes out to the angels. "Gather my saints together unto me" (Psalm 50:3–7). Evidently, many people have never seen these Scriptures. How is it that these saints aren't the same elect as seen in Matthew 24 and Mark 13? Isaiah 27:12–13 says that the children of Israel will be gathered one by one. "And it shall come to pass in that day, that the great trumpet shall be blown." The Lord shall blow the trumpet and go forth as a whirlwind—in that day. Blow the trumpet in Zion and sound an alarm in my holy mountain (Joel 2:1–2). People seem to think the trumpets only pertain to the church. I guess they missed this great trumpet and then Israel being gathered back to Jerusalem.

The Bible shows all these terms to be for Israel, but they are never said of the church. It is no coincidence that the Lord Jesus used so many of these terms in regards to the gathering of the elect in Matthew 24:31 and Mark 13:27. I believe that these phrases were given to us as clues, for all those who want to know, if only people would search out their meanings. And there is the weakness of the critics' argument, because, they have not looked at all these terms from the Old Testament. As we have seen there are many reasons why the elect, then on earth, are the Jews as it applies to Daniel's seventieth week. The church in mystery was already delivered from the wrath to come (1 Thessalonians 1:10). The church will appear with Jesus in the clouds—at the return of the King!

Then with a blast from the great trumpet, the mighty angels will go all across the world to bring sons and daughters home. We see this awesome picture, and we understand who these elect are; and we behold the mystery of the kingdom on earth unfold.

- Scattered: Leviticus 26:33; Deuteronomy 4:27–30; 30:3–4; 28:64; Hosea 9:17; Jeremiah 18:15 -17; Jeremiah 30:10–11; 31:10; Zechariah 2:6; Nehemiah 1:8–9; Isaiah 18:7; Ezekiel 11:16; 20:33–37).
- Gathered: Isaiah 11:12; Ezekiel 34:12–13; Isaiah 43:5–6; Jeremiah 23:3–5; Jeremiah 24:6; 29:14; 31:8–10; 32:37–40; Ezekiel 11:17; 20:33–37; 22:20–22; 36:24–26, 28; Deuteronomy 30:3–6; Amos 9:14–15; Zechariah 8:6–8).

Hard sayings understood by so few
It makes no sense until you study the Jew
The kingdom on earth now coming
The world and nations judged
The testimony is given, as they stand before the judge
The world now answers for how they treated
His brethren the Jews
They must now answer for how they treated the Jew
Now with the hourglass turned, with seven years the few
We now see that it is the time of the Jew

The Apocalyptic Sayings of Jesus

With so much blurredness within the telling of end times events; I thought it would be helpful to write about how some of this confusion comes about. Much of the confusion is due to replacement theology being passed off as truth, when in fact it's a departure from truth. This was a difficult chapter to write as I started out because I didn't want to leave the impression that I had the answers for all of these apocalyptic sayings, but as I started to write, the Lord gave me a peace about what I was writing. I didn't attempt to write about everything, but only the things that came to me and are left out of many end-times discussions when the apocalyptic sayings are read.

Many believers want to see the church in all of the Scriptures, and, as nice as that may seem, it can lead to confusion and misunderstanding. People actually mean well in trying to see the church in the whole New Testament, but they sometimes forget that the church didn't yet exist in the gospels and really didn't come about until after the crucifixion and the infilling of the Holy Spirit as seen in Acts. This is where people can become susceptible to replacement-theology ideas. Remember, even the disciples didn't understand that the Gentiles were to be a part of his church until Acts 15.

The disciples were still under the old covenant in the four gospels for the most part, and Jesus is seen in Matthew 10 sending out his disciples to the lost sheep of the house of Israel. They were instructed to not go to the Gentiles or any city in Samaria. Why didn't Jesus send his disciples out to the Gentiles to start a church? He didn't send them out to evangelize the Gentiles because he had to offer the earthly kingdom of heaven to the Jewish nation first, or as Jesus put it, "But go rather to the lost sheep of the house of Israel" (Matthew 10:5–7). The Jews rejected Jesus, and his disciples never really understood any of this because they were caught between the Old and New Testaments. And then Jesus started to teach about the kingdom of God, which the disciples didn't understand either. The kingdom of God reveals the bigger picture; and it takes into account the church and the things in heaven and earth, but the kingdom of heaven is the earthly kingdom. The disciples thought Jesus was going to set up the kingdom of heaven immediately. That's why Jesus then tells them of the nobleman that went into a far country, and this is how Jesus explains the postponement of the kingdom to the disciples in Luke 19:11–12.

The Mystery

The kingdom of God includes (both) things in heaven and earth.

> Having made known unto us the mystery of his will, according to his good pleasure which he hath purposed in himself: That in the dispensation of the fullness of times he might gather together in one all things in Christ, both which are in heaven, and which are on earth; even in him.
>
> Ephesians 1:9–10

Once people see that there are two programs within the plan of God, though held in mystery, then the Scriptures start making a lot more sense. Then we have the mystery of the blindness of Israel, but we are warned to not be wise in our own conceits concerning Israel. "As concerning the gospel, they are enemies for your sakes: but as touching the (election), they are beloved for the father's sake" (Romans 11:25–28). Israel will once again be God's elect on the earth after God has taken out the church from among the Gentiles a people for his name (Acts 15:14–16).

The secret mystery of the church is now revealed through the Apostle Paul by revelation. The knowledge that Gentiles shall be partakers raptured to glory with Christ is the mystery. This was not known to the sons of men ever before. It is now revealed through his holy apostles and prophets by the Spirit (Ephesians 3:1–9). The mystery of the church was hidden in God from the beginning. The prophets of old did not see this at all. It was hidden from them. Colossians 1:26–27 says, "Even the mystery which hath been hid from the ages and from generations, but now is made manifest to his saints: To whom God would make known what is the riches of the glory of this mystery among the Gentiles; which is Christ in you, the hope of glory". The mystery spoken of here is the mystery of the church and the hope we have in glory with Christ, and that hope is in heaven.

This is the mystery that the prophets didn't see, and that is why the church throughout the gospels is cloaked in mystery, because she didn't exist yet and the fact that she doesn't belong to this world. She belongs with Christ in glory. The end-time events that Jesus spoke of didn't refer to the church at all but rather to the earthly setting up of the kingdom of heaven for the Jews. The coming church age throughout the gospels was still held in mystery, but when Jesus had the twelve alone and away from the Jewish crowds, "he said unto them, Unto you it is given to know the mystery of the kingdom of God" (Mark 4:10–12). Jesus said this because he intended that they would know the mysteries after he was crucified and they would become the foundation of his church.

It's then following the death of our Lord and Savior that the disciples understood this wisdom that was not of this world. "But we speak the wisdom of God in a mystery, even the hidden wisdom, which God ordained before the world unto our glory" (1 Corinthians 2:6–7). It is with this backdrop that Paul says:

> Behold. I shew you a mystery; We shall not all sleep, but we shall all be changed, In a moment, in the twinkling of an eye, at the last trump: for the trumpet shall sound, and the dead shall be raised incorruptible, and we shall be changed. For this corruptible must put on incorruption, and this mortal must put on immortality.
>
> 1Corinthians 15:51–53

Later Paul spoke of opening his mouth boldly to make known the mystery of the gospel (Ephesians 6:19). It is interesting that Paul had just addressed married life in Ephesians 5:21–32, and in verse twenty-seven he talks of Christ presenting to himself a glorious church; and then in verse thirty-two he says, "This is a great mystery: but I speak concerning Christ and the church" (Ephesians 5:32). It is very clear that the church is presented in mystery throughout the New Testament but especially in Matthew, Mark, and Luke, where we find the apocalyptic sayings of Jesus.

This secret was not disclosed to other generations. No one had ever heard that one day the Lord would take his followers (including Gentiles) off the earth; this was a completely new concept. Not until the Apostle Paul shared about this mystery had it ever even occurred to anyone that the Lord would take believers off the earth and to heaven at the end of the age. In complete contrast to this mystery of the church, Jesus says to the Jews, "For I say unto you, Ye shall not see me henceforth, till ye shall say, Blessed is he that cometh in the name of the Lord" (Matthew 23:39). This puts the Jews on a different track and right back into the harvest scene on earth with the Feast of Tabernacles because that is what the Jews recite during the festival. They recite the Halell Psalms of 113–118 at this harvest festival, and the harvest is the end of the age. Again, you can see the two programs running alongside, the church in mystery and the Jews' earthly kingdom postponed until the end of Daniel's seventieth week when they shout, "Blessed is he who cometh in the name of the Lord." This will bring to a close the harvest threshing of man for this age.

As we get to the first apocalyptic saying of Jesus in Matthew 13:30–49, we need to understand that Jesus sent out the disciples with his message of the kingdom. We see the rejection by the Jews in Matthew 12 and the blasphemy against the Holy Spirit by the Pharisees (Matthew 12:22–32). It's almost as though it is the final straw concerning the Jews. Then starting in Matthew 13:1–17, Jesus now begins to speak about the kingdom of heaven in parables. The disciples asked him, "Why speakest thou unto them in parables? He answered and said unto them, Because it is given unto you to know the mysteries of the kingdom of heaven, but to them it is not given". This shows that the multitude of Jews would not understand, but his disciples, who would represent his church in the future, are given to know the mysteries, even if not at that time. This helps explain why Jesus keeps talking in parables to the Jews; they had rejected, and now these parables would not be understood by them. The church has been given to know the mystery that is in Christ, so as the church we can see into these parables and get a glimpse of what is going to happen to the Jews at the close of the age and the setting up of the kingdom.

Gather the Tares First

In Matthew 13:30 in reference to the Tares being gathered, Jesus says to the reapers (angels), "Gather ye together first the tares, and bind them in bundles to burn them: but gather the wheat into my barn. There is something revealed here that is very important and that is the fact that the tares or wicked shall be gathered up first. So the tares are gathered and burned at the end of (this) age. They don't even make it to the great white throne (Matthew 13:40). Jesus also says, "gather out all things that offend, and them which do iniquity" (Matthew 13:41). They will be cast into the furnace just as the beast and false prophet will be cast into the lake of fire immediately, and before the thousand-year millennium (Revelation 19:20). "So shall it be at the end of age: the angels shall come forth, and sever the wicked from among the just, And shall cast them into the furnace of fire: there shall be wailing and gnashing of teeth" (Matthew 13:49–50).

There are four distinct terms about the wicked being gathered: (1) Gather the tares first, (2) gather out all that offend, (3) and them which do iniquity, (4) sever the wicked from among the just. When we get to Matthew 24:40–42, it says something rather remarkable that many times Christians will think is the rapture of the church, but if in fact this all has to do with the earthly kingdom of the Jews being set up, then it is no surprise what this is showing. "Then shall two be in the field; the one is taken, and the other left." The one taken is taken by the angels in judgment and the same for the two women grinding at the mill: "one shall be taken, and the other left." This isn't a rapture picture; it's a judgment scene! Remember the wicked are to be severed from (among the just), meaning people will be side by side when this happens, and that is how this reads concerning the angels binding up the tares and severing the wicked.

There will be people all across the world who are still trying to survive during the profaneness of this tribulation time. Then at once the skies roll back as a brilliant light shines over Israel and the Lord appears from heaven and touches down on Mount Olivet to deal with rebellious men. Then all of a sudden, the angels appear around the world in large numbers to take away all those that offend. It is hard to even describe this time other than the most fearful thing you could ever imagine—seeing the heavens opened and the Lord returning in glory with the church and armies of heaven. The people on earth being able to see all the holy angels going forth everywhere to root out all that offend. Then the binding up of the wicked into bundles—how can one describe this scene? It is a most awesome and yet fearful time for man on earth. The ones taken are taken away and severed from among the just by the angels while they wail and gnash their teeth; then they are put into bundles with others and cast into the fire.

In the Kingdom of Their Father

"Then shall the righteous shine forth as the sun in the kingdom of their Father. Who hath ears to hear, let him hear" (Matthew 13:43). Some would think this is the church until they link this Scripture with three other Scriptures concerning the Jews. "As concerning the gospel, they are enemies for your sakes: but as touching the election, they are beloved for the father's sake" (Romans 11:28). Then we see that the righteous shall shine forth as the sun. This is revealed in Daniel 12:3, and this will be the Jews! "And they that be wise shall shine as the brightness of the firmament." This links the Jews to this passage not the church, and it is during the tribulation period seen in Daniel 12. At the judgment of the nations, "Then shall the King say unto them on his right hand, Come, ye blessed of my father, inherit the kingdom prepared for you from the foundation of the world" (Matthew 25:34). This is not the church, but the Jews inheriting the kingdom that was prepared from the foundation of the world. The church was chosen in him before the foundation of the world (Ephesians 1:4). Over and over we see the kingdom of heaven on earth for the Jews being set up all through these apocalyptic statements.

The Tribulation as Seen in Matthew 24

We need to remember the historical fact that all of the apocalyptic sayings of Jesus were spoken directly to the Jews, concerning them and the Holy City of Jerusalem, as predicted in Daniel 9:24. They were not spoken to the church or the Gentiles. The church did not yet exist, and as shown before, the church is seen in mystery throughout the New Testament.

Another thing to remember is that after their rejection and from then on, Jesus spoke to the Jews in parables because it was not given to them to know the mysteries of the kingdom of heaven. Jesus told his followers privately and away from the crowds that they alone would understand the mysteries (Matthew 13:3, 10–11; Mark 4:10–13). Except for the disciples: "All these things spake Jesus unto the multitude in parables; and without a parable spake he not unto them" (Matthew 13:34).

The twenty-fourth chapter of Matthew seems to show the first and second half of the tribulation. (There are similarities in the Olivet discourse in Matthew 24:4–14, and with Revelation 6, it shows that they are addressing the same period of time, the first three and half years of the tribulation.)

Starting with Matthew 24:4, Jesus says, "take heed that no man deceive you." Well, starting out in Revelation 6, we see the anti-christ coming forth to conquer with the opening of the first seal, and he will definitely deceive the Jews, for Jesus said, "I am come in my Father's name, and ye receive me not: If another shall come in his own name him ye will receive" (John 5:43).

First deception, then war comes to the earth. "And ye shall hear of wars and rumours of wars. For nation shall rise against nation, and kingdom against kingdom" (Matthew 24:6–7). With the opening of the second seal in Revelation 6, we see peace taken from the earth. "And there went out another horse that was red: and power was given to him that sat thereon to take peace from the earth, and that they should kill one another: and there was given unto him a great sword" (Revelation 6:4). Notice how closely all these things seem to connect to Matthew 24:4–14.

Matthew 24:7 says, "and there shall be famines." Then, with the opening of the third seal, we see famine upon the earth. "A measure of wheat for a penny, and three measures of barley for a penny" (Revelation 6:5–6).

"Then shall they deliver you up to be afflicted, and shall kill you" (Matthew 24:9). With the opening of the fourth seal, we see the rider on the pale horse: "and his name that sat on him was Death, and Hell followed with him." This rider kills a fourth part of the earth (Revelation 6:8)!

On the heels of the fourth seal and with the opening of the fifth seal, we see the martyrs are killed (Revelation 6:9). "And shall kill you: and ye shall be hated of all nations for my name's sake" (Matthew 24:9). I believe that those killed will be Jews and Gentiles who missed the rapture and now believe in Christ. The martyrs killed are killed for their witness of Jesus (Revelation 20:4).

"And this gospel of the kingdom shall be preached in all the world for a witness unto all nations; and then shall the end come" (Matthew 24:14). This gospel of the kingdom is referring once again to the earthly kingdom on earth. The church cloaked in mystery is already in heaven, and that's why the gospel of the kingdom is again the earthly kingdom that the Lord is about to set up through the Jews.

Matthew 24:3–14 is the first three and half years of the tribulation, known as the beginning of sorrows (Matthew 24:8). The tribulation period of seven years, or Daniel's seventieth week, includes the beginning of sorrows as we see here in the first part of Matthew up to verse fourteen. And then the great tribulation starts: "When ye shall see the abomination of desolation, spoken of by Daniel the prophet, stand in the holy place, (whoso readeth, let him understand) (Matthew 24:15–31).

Second Half of Tribulation

Called the Great Tribulation, Matthew 24:15

The second half of the tribulation starts when the antichrist goes into the temple to declare himself God in the face of all. This is the abomination of desolation spoken of in Matthew 24:15. We also know that when this happens as seen in Revelation 13:5 the antichrist will have only forty-two months from that point, and forty-two months is three and a half years. The rest of Matthew 24:15–31 shows the Jews dealing with all this from the land of Israel and those in Judea are to flee to the mountains. Please see the chapter on the elect, because it covers most of the terminology from verses sixteen to thirty-one as it pertains to:

The Jews will see the abomination of desolation go into the temple.
The Jews in Judea fleeing to the mountains
Praying that their flight be not on the Sabbath
The sun being darkened (Christians will not be in darkness)
Israel being gathered in the dark and cloudy day
Then the Son of man appearing in the clouds (see Son-of-man chapter)
The great sound of a trumpet
The Son of man sending forth his angels (to bring the Jews back to Jerusalem)
Then shall two be in the field, the one taken the other left (this is a judgment scene)
Gathering the elect from one end of heaven to the other

Matthew 25:31–41

The Olivet Discourse Continues

Judgment of the Nations

"When the Son of man shall come in his glory, and all the holy angels with him, (then) shall he sit upon throne of his glory" (Matthew 19:28). The Lamb had stood up in Revelation 5:6 and through the tribulation of Daniel's seventieth week, and now he is seen sitting again to judge the nations. "And before him shall be gathered all nations: and he shall separate them one from another, as a shepherd divideth his sheep from the goats" (Matthew 25:31–32). "Let the heathen be awakened, and come up to the valley of Jehoshaphat: for there will I sit to judge the heathen round about"

(Joel 3:12). Verses thirteen through sixteen go on to talk about the harvest of the wicked and how the sun and moon are darkened as it's linked to Matthew 24:29–31.

This judgment of the nations is from Israel in the valley of Jehoshaphat, but it is also clear that the angels are sent out at this time to sever the wicked from among the just, all around the world as spoken in Matthew 13:49–50. The one shall be taken, the other left.

Mark 13:7–27

Olivet Discourse Continues

These passages are very similar to Matthew 24. One of the differences is found in Mark 13:9 where it says, "But take heed to yourselves: for they shall deliver you up to councils; and in the synagogues ye shall be beaten: and ye shall be brought before rulers and kings for my sake, for a testimony against them". As it was during the days of Nazi Germany when the Jews were persecuted all throughout Europe, we now see an even greater persecution of the Jews but on a worldwide scale. The synagogues are mentioned because this all has to do with the Jews. Mark 13:12 indicates that this will be a time when the Jewish people will turn on each other. The pressures and deception of the antichrist will set families against each other. The main point seems to be that the Jews will be brought before rulers for his name's sake (Mark 13:9–13).

The Lord will judge all people and nations as to how they treated the Jews, especially during the tribulation period. "And the King shall answer and say unto them, Verily I say unto you, Inasmuch as ye have done it unto one of the least of these my brethren, ye have done it unto me" (Matthew 25:40). This is how the world is judged at that time of the Second Coming. It will be how people and nations treat his brethren the Jews during Daniel's seventieth week. There is no hint of the church in this at all, only the earthly kingdom as it relates to the Jews. The time of grace ended seven years prior when the Lamb stood up with the twenty-four elders present and opened the first seal (Revelation 5:6). Notice how replacement theology ideas all of a sudden look bankrupt once people begin seeing how these apocalyptic statements concern the

Jews and the setting up of the earthly kingdom at the end of the tribulation.

Luke 17:24–37

Verse twenty-four says, "For as the lightning, that lighteneth out of the one part under heaven, shineth unto the other part under heaven; so shall also the Son of man be in his day." This indicates that there will be a singular light that shines from a part of heaven or sky but it will illuminate to the other parts under heaven. It is very important to note also that "so shall also the Son of man be in his day." Notice how "in his day" is singular; this shows that the coming of the Lord is on a day, meaning a singular day.

Now notice the change as it pertains to Noe. "And as it was in the days of Noe, so shall it be also in the days of the Son of man. They did eat, they drank, they married wives, they were given in marriage, until the day that Noe entered into the ark, and the flood came, and destroyed them all" (Luke 17:26–27). We see that the word now is days in verse twenty-six. It is no longer called a day in the singular; it uses days twice showing it to be a time period. This helps set forth the timing for the people on earth, and yes, people will at the start of the seven-year tribulation or Daniel's seventieth week begin by eating and drinking and marrying, just as they did in the days of Noe. Notice what happened to the people on earth on the seventh day of the flood. "And it came to pass after seven days, that the waters of the flood were upon the earth" (Genesis 7:10). This means that they too were eating and drinking and marrying until the seventh day and the flood was upon the earth and finally engulfed them.

Some people say that this can't picture the tribulation because there is no way people can be eating and drinking and given in marriage with all the things in Revelation being done upon the earth. They forget that these days represent a time period of seven years in the book of Revelation. At the start of the tribulation, the whole world will wonder after the beast for three and a half years into the tribulation (Revelation 13:3–5). The tribulation starts out with the rider on the white horse, or a false peace, as seen in Revelation 6:2. Daniel's seventieth week is foreshadowed in the flood account in Genesis 7:10, and Jesus links that time with the end of the age. "And it came to pass after seven days, that the waters of the flood were upon the earth." Obviously, the seven days started out not so bad; they were eating and drinking until at some point on the seventh day of the tribulation of the flood they were all destroyed. The seven-year tribulation starts with a false peace, with people around the world deceived by the antichrist. They will eat and drink and even marry and by the seventh day as seen in Noe's flood or the seventh year, as seen in the book of Revelation they will all be destroyed (Luke 17:27).

Luke 21:7–36

Olivet Discourse Continues

As this starts out, it continues with many of the similarities already mentioned in the apocalypse. There will be wars, and nation rising against nation and even kingdom against kingdom. Verse eleven talks about great earthquakes, famines, and pestilence and then it says, "and fearful sights and great signs shall there be from heaven" (Luke 21:11). Men will no longer be able to see the stars at night, and even the moon and the sun will be darkened.

> For the stars of heaven and the constellations thereof shall not give their light: the sun shall be darkened in his going forth, and the moon shall not cause her light to shine. And I will punish the world for their evil, and the wicked for their iniquity; and I will cause the arrogance of the proud to cease, and will lay low the haughtiness of the terrible.
>
> Isaiah 13:10–11

"Therefore I will shake the heavens, and the earth shall remove out of her place, in the wrath of the Lord of hosts, and in the day of his anger" (Isaiah 13:13). All these statements help explain that "fearful sights and great signs shall there be from heaven."

Scripture goes on to talk about the Jews being delivered up to the synagogues and being betrayed by their friends and family. This is all about the Jews being betrayed and brought before synagogues, kings, and rulers. This again shows how the people of the world are to be judged at that time. They will be judged by how they treated the brethren of Jesus, the Jews, and this is such a paradigm shift as compared to Christianity's grace and to when the church was on the earth. This helps to explain this time period of Daniel's seventieth week and how the world will be judged by its treatment of the Jews. It's then that these apocalyptic statements start to make sense in light of the kingdom of heaven.

Luke 21:20 says, "And when ye shall see Jerusalem compassed with armies, then know that the desolation thereof is nigh." More warnings to the Jews about what they are to do. "Then let them which are in Judea flee to the mountains; and let them which are in the midst of it depart out; and let not them that are in the countries enter there into" (Luke 21:21). The Jews are to flee out of the city of Jerusalem. This has nothing to do with the church fleeing into the mountains; no, this is the same story of the Jews' earthly kingdom being set up and what happens to the Jews and Jerusalem at that time.

"For these be the days of vengeance, that all things which are written may be fulfilled" (Luke 21:22). "For there shall be great distress in the land, and wrath upon this people" (Luke 21:23). What land are we talking about other than Israel, and what people are under wrath at this time other than the Jews? This is all clearly seen as happening to the Jews in the land of Israel. Luke 21:24 says, "And they shall fall by the edge of the sword, and shall be led away captive into all nations." This is the Jews who are killed by the edge of the sword, and it is the Jews who are led away captive into all nations at this time. "And Jerusalem shall be trodden down of the Gentiles, until the times of the Gentiles be fulfilled" (Luke 21:24). It is the Holy City of Jerusalem that will be trodden down, not cities in America.

Moving forward to the end of Luke 21:36: "Watch ye therefore, and pray always, that ye may be accounted worthy to escape all these things that shall come to pass, and to stand before the Son of man". This is a great Scripture that shows the Jews in this time period and that they are to pray that they might stand before the Son of man. This could never be the church because we will see the Son of God not the Son of man; we will see him seven years prior to this event happening. The church believes in the Son of God, and the term Son of man doesn't apply to the church. Only those left on earth at his coming will see the coming of the Son of man. The church will appear with him in glory (Colossians 3:4).

In summary of the apocalyptic sayings of Jesus, we see that in the gospels of Matthew, Mark, and Luke the church did not yet exist. Jesus had not yet died, and the veil was not yet torn in two. Jesus sent the disciples out to the lost sheep of Israel and not to the Gentiles (Matthew 10). In the Jews' rejection of Jesus and the kingdom of heaven, then Jesus proceeds to talk to the Jews from then on in parables (Matthew 13).

The kingdom of heaven is then postponed, and only the followers of Jesus would understand the mysteries. The Jews still don't see any of this to this day, but the church as followers of Christ can know the mysteries. The church is veiled in mystery all through Matthew, Mark, and Luke. Then the Apostle Paul makes known the mystery that had never before been revealed, not even to the prophets, the great mystery of the church including Gentiles one day being changed in an instant and taken to heaven. Then in the fullness of times, Christ will bring both things together, those in heaven with those on earth, even in him (Ephesians 1:10).

So then all of the apocalyptic sayings are seen having everything to do with the Jews as the elect on earth. With the time of grace having ended, the people on earth will then be directly held accountable for how they treated the Jews during Daniel's seventieth week. This is why everything focuses on the Jews because they will be persecuted for a testimony against all those who hate Christ and his brethren the Jews. Then the King will sit to judge, and the testimony will be heard against the nations. This brings to close the end of the age, the time of man on earth is changing, changing into the kingdom age. The kingdom of heaven on earth now begins. The millennium age springs forth, and the meek shall inherit the earth. I hope this study helps to explain some of the end-time statements made in the synoptic gospels of Matthew, Mark, and Luke.

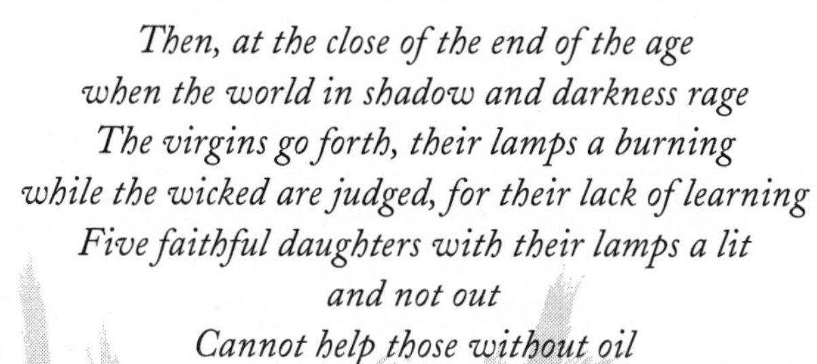

Then, at the close of the end of the age
when the world in shadow and darkness rage
The virgins go forth, their lamps a burning
while the wicked are judged, for their lack of learning
Five faithful daughters with their lamps a lit
and not out
Cannot help those without oil
For they have run out

The Ten Virgins

The ten virgins is a topic that has some very interesting aspects to it concerning the end times. It has nothing to do with the rapture of the church, but it does help us to get a sense of what's happening on earth at the Lord's return. It focuses right back on the Jews and how they are seen as the virgin daughters of Zion. I had asked a Jewish Rabbi about what the term "virgin daughters of Zion" means. He told me it was a poetic reference for the children of Israel. This chapter points out the everlasting covenant they have as the virgin daughters of Zion. The day of the Lord is looked at in this study; it is a time of darkness. Having one's lamp lit in the east would also keep out serpents and the implication of what that means as it is seen during the day of the Lord. The Jews will go forth having their lamps lit, and they will go forth in the day of darkness.

Who are the ten virgins in Matthew chapter twenty-five? Some teach that this parable is a warning to be ready; but there is one little word that gets overlooked when studying about the ten virgins, and the word is *then* (shall the kingdom of heaven be likened unto ten virgins). The word then is inserted here to help us understand what had just been revealed by Jesus. You have all the apocalyptic sayings told by Jesus in chapter twenty-four in answer to his disciples' question of when the end of the age would be. This helps us understand that this picture of the ten virgins follows all of those things concerning the end of the age. So then, what does this picture establish? Is it Israel that is warned to be ready with their lamps burning?

"Then shall the kingdom of heaven be likened unto ten virgins, which took their lamps, and went forth to meet the bridegroom" (Matthew 25:1). Jesus identifies himself in Luke 5:34–35, as the bridegroom. Even John the Baptist identifies Jesus as the bridegroom in John 3:29. "He that hath the bride is the bridegroom: But the friend of the bridegroom, which standeth and heareth him, rejoiceth greatly because of the bridegroom's voice: This my joy therefore is fulfilled". John the Baptist could say this because he was standing there listening to Jesus, the bridegroom. Luke 12:35–36 says, "Let your loins be girded about, and your lights burning; And ye yourselves like unto men that wait for their Lord, when he will return from the wedding; that when he cometh and knocketh, they may open unto him immediately." This is a message to the Jews to watch and be ready: "Blessed are those servants." Jesus calls the church friends, so we know he is not referring to the church here in Luke 12:35–36. Notice how when the bridegroom returns he will have already taken his wife (Revelation 19:7–9, Luke 12:36). Obviously, these virgins in Matthew 25 cannot be the church because the church is coming back with the bridegroom.

What does it mean that the foolish took their lamps and took no oil? But the wise took oil in their vessels with their lamps? Concerning the day of the Lord, the Scripture says something very interesting in Zephaniah 1:12. "It will come about at that time, that I will search Jerusalem with lamps. And I will punish the men who are stagnant in spirit, who say in their hearts, The Lord will not do good nor evil" (NAS). Notice that this is the prophetic time period of the day of the Lord. It is a time of darkness and wrath (verses twelve through eighteen). The King James Version says, "I will search Jerusalem with candles, and punish the men that are settled on their lees." How does this apply to the ten virgins?

Lees

In Wilson Old Testament Word Studies,10 it says, "lees of wine, so called because wine kept, preserved in strength and colour, by letting it stand on the lees." (Jeremiah 48:11, Zephaniah 1:12). To rest upon one's lees is to live a life of quiet indifference (Isaiah 25:6). The dregs at the bottom of wine jars.11 Lees, from a word meaning to keep or preserve. It was applied to Lees from the custom of allowing wine to stand on the lees. Men settled on lees are men "hardened or crusted." The effect of wealthy undisturbed ease on the ungodly is hardening. They become stupidly secure (Psalm 55:19, Amos 6:1.12

Job 12:5 says something interesting that connects the lamp and those settled on their lees. "He that is ready to slip with his feet is as a lamp despised in the thought of him that is at ease." (Despised is a Lamp gone out). He that is at ease is one quietly indifferent or one settled on their lees (the five foolish virgins).

The importance of the burning lamp is pointed out for the children of Israel in the book of Exodus.

> And thou shalt command the children of Israel, that they bring thee pure oil olive beaten for the light, to cause the lamp to burn always. In the tabernacle of the congregation without the veil, which is before the testimony, Aaron and his sons shall order it from evening to morning before the Lord: It shall be a statute forever unto their generation on the behalf of the children of Israel.
>
> Exodus 27:20–21

We see that it was the Lord that commanded the children of Israel to keep their lamps lit always, and always means always. For the Jews to become indifferent, they would then have to become as wine on the lees and their lamps have gone out (the five foolish).

"In the East, a lamp or flame is appealed to for confirmation of a covenant, which is thought to explain Genesis 15:17. Job 12:5 indicates that a lamp or torch, despised, is a lamp that has ceased to burn. Lamps in the East were kept burning all night" (Wilson Old Testament Word Studies). There is a very interesting reason why this may have been so. A lamp lit would also keep the snakes out of people's homes, an interesting concept. In Amos 5:17–20, it mentions a man leaning on the wall of his home only to be bitten by a serpent. It begs the question, if that same man had his lamp lit, would he have been bit by the serpent? It is also interesting that it is mentioned with the time of judgment, or the day of the Lord (the foolish virgins).

The candle (or lamp) of the wicked shall be put out (Job 18:5–6; 21:17). Also, Proverbs 13:9, 13 says, "The light of the righteous rejoices: But the lamp of the wicked shall be put out." Whosoever despises the word shall be destroyed (the five foolish or indifferent virgins).

(Wisdom Personified)
She hath mixed her wine
She hath sent out her maidens
Come eat my food and drink of the wine I have mixed
Forsake your folly and live
Proverbs 9:1–6

A call to the Daughters of Zion?

The vineyard of the Lord of hosts is the house of Israel (Isaiah 5:2–7). Israel is also likened to grapes in the wilderness (Hosea 9:10). The sin of Moab was that he was proud.

> Moab hath been at ease from his youth, and he hath settled on his lees, and hath not been emptied from vessel to vessel, neither hath he gone into captivity: therefore, behold, the days come, saith the Lord, that I will send unto him wanderers, and shall cause him to wander, and shall empty his vessels, and break their bottles.
>
> Jeremiah 48:11–12

Moab was likened to wine on the lees, or one that is stagnant and indifferent to the things of God. "The Lord hath trodden the virgin, the daughter of Judah, as in a wine press" (Lamentation 1:15). The foolish that say in their heart, "The Lord will not do good, neither will he do evil" (Zephaniah 1:12). They are as foolish virgins with their lamps gone out. They have become stagnant or indifferent. They are become as wine on the lees, the basest or least desirable (the five foolish). "The Lord will search Jerusalem with lamps in that day and all the sinners of Israel shall die by the sword, which say, The evil shall not overtake nor prevent us" (Amos 9:10). "The Lord of Hosts will make unto all people a feast of fat things, a feast of wines on the lees, of fat things full of marrow, of wines on the lees well refined" (Isaiah 25:6).

> I have trodden the winepress alone; and of the people there was none with me: for I will tread them in mine anger, and trample them in my fury; and their blood shall be sprinkled upon my garments, and I will stain all my raiment. For the day of vengeance is in mine heart, and the year of my redeemed is come.
>
> Isaiah 63:3–4

> For in the hand of the LORD there is a cup, and the wine is red; it is full of mixture; and he poureth out of the same: but the dregs thereof, all the wicked of the earth shall wring them out, and drink them. But I will declare for ever; I will sing praises to the God of Jacob.
>
> Psalm 75:8–9

This is an awesome description of judgment upon all peoples and even upon the virgin daughters of Jerusalem (the five foolish). The five wise will go forth with their lamps lit.

The heart of the Father toward Jerusalem is revealed in Isaiah 62:1, where it says, "For Zion's sake will I not hold my peace, and for Jerusalem's sake I will not rest, until the righteousness thereof go forth as brightness, and the salvation thereof as a lamp that burneth". This shows that the Lord is looking forward to that day when the five wise virgins go forth to meet their Lord with their lamps lit during the day of darkness.

"For thus saith the Lord unto the House of Israel, Seek ye me, and ye shall live" (Amos 5:4). The five wise virgins shall seek him with their lamps lit. That is because the day of the Lord shall be darkness. The five foolish do not believe the Lord will do good or evil. They are like wine on the lees, or a lamp despised and gone out. "And in all vineyards shall be wailing: for I will pass through thee, saith the Lord. Woe unto you that desire the day of the Lord! To what end is for you? The day of the Lord is darkness, and not light" (Amos 5:17–20). It's as if they have been bit by that cunning serpent; and woe to them that are indifferent in Zion (Amos 6:1).

The ten virgins is a picture of those Jews that believe and are waiting for their Lord and those that are indifferent to him.

Why the Ten Virgins are Not the Church

1. The ten virgins go forth to meet the bridegroom after the wedding. But the Lord will be returning with his bride; the church cannot be on the earth at that time (Revelation 19:7–8, 14; Zechariah 14:5; Colossians 3:4; 1Thessalonians 3:13; 4:14; Jude 14).
2. The oil in Matthew 25 concerning the ten virgins is not referring to the Holy Spirit. Most people just assume that every time oil is mentioned in the Bible it is referring to the Holy Spirit. The Holy Spirit cannot be purchased. It is unwise for anyone to suggest that Jesus was implying that the Holy Spirit can be bought or purchased. Jesus is the Word made flesh, and he is not going to contradict the Scriptures. In Acts 8:18–24 Simon offers Peter money so that he can lay hands on people. Peter then says to Simon, "Thy money perish with thee, because thou hast thought that the gift of God may be purchased with money." This lays to rest any reference to the oil being the Holy Spirit in Matthew 25. I believe that this reference for oil comes after the Holy Spirit has taken the church up in the rapture; therefore, the oil is now literal when it talks about oil in the lamps.
3. If you have the Holy Spirit, you cannot lose him. Jesus said, "I will never leave you or forsake you" (Hebrews 13:5). This also lays to rest that you can somehow run out of the Holy Spirit. Therefore, these virgins cannot be Christians.
4. There is a picture of the Jews waiting for their Lord with their lights burning, in Luke 12:35–37. It talks about the Lord returning from the wedding and they, the Jews, waiting. Blessed are those servants. The church is referred to as friends, not servants, and the fact that the church returns with the Lord at that time shows us that these are the children of Israel, and for that matter you could call them the virgin Daughters of Zion.

The Virgin Daughters of Zion

In Jeremiah 6:2, it speaks of the daughter of Zion as not hearkening to the truth (the five foolish?). "The comely and dainty one, the daughter of Zion, I will cut off." The reason they are cut off is seen in verses eight through ten: "Behold their ear is uncircumcised, and they cannot hearken: Behold, the word of the Lord is unto them a reproach; they have no delight in it." This is a clear picture of what will happen to those virgins who have let their lamps go out. Isaiah 62:11 speaks of the Lord's return and declares to the daughter of Zion that the Lord will return, and his reward will be with him. "Say ye to the daughter of Zion, behold his reward is with him" (Isaiah 62:11, Revelation 22:12).

Micah chapter four lays it out clearly concerning, the last days and how it affects the daughters of Zion and how the kingdom will come to her. In verse eight it points out that the kingdom shall come, and you could put in "the five wise virgins" there when you read it. "And thou, O tower of the flock, the strong hold of the daughter of Zion, unto thee shall it come, even the first dominion; The kingdom shall come to the daughter of Jerusalem" (Micah 4:8).

The term "the kingdom shall come to the daughter of Jerusalem" confirms the timing; in the last days it shall come to pass and in that day or the Day of the Lord.

Now when we look at Matthew 25, it becomes apparent that the daughters of Zion are like ten virgins, which took their lamps and went forth to meet the bridegroom. As we have seen, Jesus is the bridegroom, and when he returns he will already have taken his bride. He will be returning from the wedding (Luke 12:36, Revelation 19:7–14).

There is a promise for the daughters of Zion in Zephaniah 3:14–17, and if you prefer you could say, "the five wise virgins." "Sing, O daughter of Zion; shout, O Israel; be glad and rejoice with all the heart, O daughter of Jerusalem." Verses sixteen through twenty show the time in the end when the Lord will rejoice over Jerusalem and the daughters of Zion. "The Lord thy God in the midst of thee is mighty; he will save, he will rejoice over thee with joy; he will rest in his love, he will joy over thee with singing." Zechariah 2:10–12 says, "Sing O daughter of Zion; for, lo, I come, and I will dwell in the midst of thee, saith the Lord." In that day, he will utter his voice from Jerusalem (Joel 3:15–16, Isaiah 2:3–5).

Zechariah 9:9 says, "Rejoice greatly, O daughter of Zion; shout, O daughter of Jerusalem: behold thy King cometh unto thee: he is just and having salvation; lowly, and riding upon an ass, and upon a colt the foal of an ass". Jesus came into Jerusalem, and they received him not. When he comes again in that day, it will be a day of darkness, and the believing Jews will go forth with their lamps lit. They will be as servants that wait for their Lord that when he comes they may open unto him immediately. Make no mistake; they will have their lamps lit because it is to show the everlasting covenant toward them to all generations. "For Jerusalem's sake the Lord will not rest, until the righteousness thereof go forth as brightness, and the salvation thereof as a lamp that burneth" (Isaiah 62:1). Here is a beautiful picture set before us of the daughters of Zion or the five wise virgins going forth to meet their Lord at the end of the tribulation. The ten virgins cannot be the church.

The earthly kingdom comes
The promises to the father's fulfilled
The head and not the tail
Those who will not serve thee shall perish in the way
As the towers fall and the rivers of water flow
They flow down from the mountains, where the sun is now sevenfold
Then the King heals the stroke of their wound
This same King they see, with the wounds in his hands
Has healed up their wounds and here he stands
In bitterness they cry, as for an only son
They've been brought through the fire, purified as gold
Then the King says they are his, and the people shout
The Lord is my God, and we will never go out!

Israel's Earthly Kingdom

Israel's earthly kingdom is coming, but this is something not genuinely understood by many Christians. As Christians, we sometimes forget that Israel has been promised her land forever, and as the chapter on the apocalyptic sayings of Jesus justly noted, Israel will be involved in the kingdom of heaven on earth. Once Christians start to think they are Israel and have somehow assimilated Israel's promises, then bad doctrine and error are not far behind. It can also encourage vengefulness against Israel, and this is tragic because we are called upon to pray for the peace of Jerusalem. We need to understand Israel's place into eternity is upon the earth, and it's our place to be in heaven with the Lord. There are different destinies for different people found throughout the Scriptures. This chapter will hopefully stir a love for Israel and light the way to help establish some basic facts about what God has promised for Israel.

God has a glorious plan for all believers throughout all the long ages, a noble plan that is sometimes different depending on what covenant the people came under at the time they lived. "The Bible is God's one and only book. In it he discloses facts of eternity as well as of time, of heaven and hell as well as of earth, of himself as well as of his creatures, and of his purposes in all creation. The reader of the Scriptures should be prepared to discover revelation which at times deals with other beings and their destiny quite apart from himself."13

There are different groups of people, from former times and from different ages that are found throughout the Scriptures, these being the Jews, the Gentiles, and the church. In fact, there are three more groups, the Old Testament saints, the tribulation saints, and the 144,000 Jews who are seen in heaven in Revelation 14:1–3. These last three groups either came before the church or after the church was raptured, but they are not the church. Each group has an eternal destiny that the Scripture reveals that are all quite different from each other. In this study, we will look at Israel's earthly kingdom. It will be those Jews that endure until the end and are alive at the time when Jesus comes back to the Mount of Olives (Matthew 24:13). These Jews are the ones who will go into the kingdom along with the Gentiles, or as they are referred to, as sheep, on the right hand, the ones who survive the tribulation and make it through the judgment of the nations. Those are the people that will inherit the kingdom prepared from the foundation of the world (Matthew 25:34).

Although this chapter is about Israel, it must be stated that the church was chosen in him before the foundation of the world (Ephesians 1:4). You could also say it this way: those going into the kingdom on earth were chosen since the overthrow, and when talking about the church you could say we were chosen in him before the overthrow. This is the old way of pointing out when sin entered our world, and in the church's case how we were chosen before the fall, because we have the better covenant. Different groups were chosen for different destinies, depending on the covenant from God they come under. This also helps to show that there is a very real difference between covenants. It is easily established that the church has a better covenant established by the better promises as stated in Hebrews 8:6. The church has a heavenly destiny established upon it.

The promises for Israel however are earthly.

> The distinction between the purpose of Israel and the purpose for the church is about as important as that which exists between the two Testaments. Every covenant, promise, and provision for Israel is earthly, and they continue as a nation with the earth when it is created new. Every covenant or promise for the church is for a heavenly reality, and she continues in heavenly citizenship when the heavens are recreated.14

When talking about the church, we understand that we have never been promised any land like the nation of Israel. Despite what we may think on these matters, this all has to do with the divine providence of God and the plan he has set in motion for the ages.

With a mighty proclamation from the Lord, Israel receives an eternal promise to the land. "For all the land which thou seest, to thee will I give it, and to thy seed forever" (Genesis 13:15). It is rather alarming to realize that many people today are contradicting Scripture and they are now saying that those promises were not meant forever, and that is dangerous. We see this drama played out even today as Israel continues to struggle for her very existence. It is fitting that the whole world is against Israel because the earthly kingdoms are ruled by Satan. Right now Israel is sidetracked until the Lord takes out a people for his name, the church.

Isaiah 60:21 says, "Thy people also shall be all righteous; They shall inherit the land forever, the branch of my planting, the work of my hands, that I may be glorified". They shall inherit the land and an eternal kingdom will be set up. Daniel 2:44 says, "And in the days of these kings shall the God of heaven set up a kingdom, which shall never be destroyed: and the kingdom shall not be left to other people, but it shall break in pieces and consume all these kingdoms, and it shall stand forever". The Lord says it shall not be left to other people. So it is foolishness for anyone including Christians to act as though we have somehow supplanted Israel. We need to understand that the church is under a different covenant. Christians should actually know better than to think that they are going to be on the earth when our Lord told us that we are not of this world (John 15:19; 17:16).

> And David my servant shall be king over them; and they all shall have one shepherd: they shall also walk in my judgments, and observe my statues, and do them. And they shall dwell in the land that I have given unto Jacob my servant, wherein your fathers have dwelt; and they shall dwell therein, even they, and their children, and their children's children forever: and my servant David shall be their prince forever.
>
> Ezekiel 37:24–25

In Luke 1:31–33 we see Jesus will sit on the throne of David, and we already know that the church will share in this reign.

Israel's kingdom then is rightfully of the earth, so when Jesus ultimately takes his bride, the church, out of this world, he then changes course to deal with Israel.

> Simeon hath declared how God at the first did visit the Gentiles, to take out of them a people for his name. And to this agree the words of the prophets; as it is written, After this I will return, and will build again the tabernacle of David, which is fallen down; and I will build again the ruins thereof, and I will set it up.
>
> Acts 15:14–16

This shows the change in the dispensation age that follows the church, from the age of grace right into Daniel's seventieth week, a time determined upon thy people and the Holy City.

It is then that God turns to reckon with Israel, (again) meaning they have been sidetracked until the Lord takes out a people for his name. The timing here is important to understand because it is after the rapture that this will happen. It is then that he causes the Jews to pass under the rod and will purge out the rebels of Israel (Ezekiel 20:37–38). This is referring to the tribulation period. "Alas! for that day is great, so that none is like it: it is even the time of Jacob's trouble; but he shall be saved out of it" (Jeremiah 30:7). This is Daniel's seventieth week, or the last seven years. How can we know it's seven years? It's not that complex to understand when you see the antichrist go into the temple in midweek and causes the sacrifice to cease (Daniel 9:27). And then there's forty-two months, or three and one half years left (Daniel 12:11, Revelation 13:5–18).

It's not the aim of this chapter to show what happens in the tribulation period other than tracing Israel's earthly destiny. It is evident that God is going to fulfill his plans for Israel, and the church has not replaced Israel in anyway; we have a different covenant. All the people and nations left on earth will (then) be judged in a radically different way to what the world has known and seen through the church age of grace. The world will now be held into account by a holy God, as to how they treated the brethren of Jesus, the Jews. Whole nations and individuals will have to give an account before the King for everything they did or didn't do for the Jewish nation. Many times when reading the gospels this fact is overlooked, and especially as it concerns the judgment of the nations (Matthew 25:41–46).

During the judgment of the nations, Joel 3:2 says, "I will also gather all nations, and will bring them down into the valley of Jehoshaphat, and will plead with them there for my people and for my heritage Israel, whom they have scattered among the nations, and parted my land". In view of the fact that we are talking about Israel in her earthly setting, we see the statement by the Lord that Israel is his heritage, and it is clear that it is upon the earth. Zechariah 14 shows the nations gathered against Jerusalem to battle, and in that day his feet shall stand upon the Mount of Olives. Verse five says, "and the Lord my God shall come and all the saints with thee." These are the ancients of the church and Old Testament saints coming back to earth on white horses in victory, as the armies of heaven, even the angels (Revelation 19:7–14; Daniel 7:13–14; Zechariah 14:4–5; Colossians 3:4; 1 Thessalonians 3:13; 4:14; Jude 14; Isaiah 24:21–23).

It is at this time that "The sun and the moon shall be darkened, and the stars shall withdraw their shining." That's when "The Lord will roar out of Zion, and utter His voice from Jerusalem; and the heavens and the earth shall shake: but the Lord will be the hope of His people, and the strength of the children of Israel" (Joel 3:15–16). The church will come back with him, and the apostles will sit on twelve thrones judging Israel. But for the Gentiles he shall judge among the nations and shall rebuke many people in the valley of Jehoshaphat (Joel 3:12–16). "And He shall judge among many people, and rebuke strong nations afar off; and they shall beat their swords into plowshares, and their spears into pruning hooks" (Micah 4:1–3).

> And many nations shall come, and say, Come ye, and let us go up to the mountain of the Lord, and to the house of the God of Jacob; and He will teach us of His ways, and we will walk in his paths: for the law shall go forth of Zion, and the word of the Lord from Jerusalem.
>
> Isaiah 2:3–4,12–16

Some people erroneously believe that the Lord will somehow judge Christians when he judges the nations. Matthew 25:34 is talking about those nations that the Lord shall separate at his coming, not that these are Christians, for the church was previously caught up and we have already thrown our crowns before the throne, way back in Revelation 4. The nations will be judged for how they treated his brethren, the Jews, during the tribulation period (Matthew 25:34–46). These people of Matthew 25:34 will inherit the kingdom prepared for them from the foundation of the world. This shows again that the church has a better covenant, which was established upon better promises (Hebrews 8:6–7). The church will sit in heavenly places (Ephesians 2:6).

When the Lord comes back,

> And in that day it shall come to pass, that he that is left in Zion, and he that remaineth in Jerusalem, shall be called holy, even everyone that is written among the living in Jerusalem: When the Lord shall have washed away the filth of the daughters of Zion, and shall have purged the blood of Jerusalem from the midst thereof by the spirit of judgment, and by the spirit of burning.
>
> Isaiah 4:3–4

"At that time will I bring you again, even in the time that I gather you: for I will make you a name and a praise among the people of the earth, when I turn back your captivity before your eyes, saith the Lord" (Zephaniah 3:14–20). This is a glorious proclamation from the Lord to the Jewish nation and the fact that he will bless them the more on earth. And to this purpose we say; long may he shine upon them.

> And it shall come to pass in that day, that I will seek to destroy all the nations that come against Jerusalem. And I will pour upon the house of David, and upon the inhabitants of Jerusalem, the spirit of grace and of supplications: and they shall look upon me whom they have pierced, and they shall mourn for him, as one mourneth

> for His only son, and shall be in bitterness for him, as one that is in bitterness for his firstborn.
>
> Zechariah 12:9–10

It is hard to imagine the thoughts of wonder that will flood through the minds of the children of Israel in that day. On the day when all their troubles shall vanish away.

> And there shall be upon every high mountain, and upon every high hill, rivers and streams of water in the day of the great slaughter, when the towers fall. Moreover the light of the moon shall be as the light of the sun, and the light of the sun shall be sevenfold, as the light of seven days, in the day that the LORD bindeth up the breach of his people, and healeth the stroke of their wound.
>
> Isaiah 30:25–26

The purpose and the promises for Israel will shine out the clearer on that day when, "the moon shall be confounded, and the sun ashamed, when the LORD of hosts shall reign in mount Zion, and in Jerusalem and before his ancients gloriously" (Isaiah 24:21–23; Daniel 7:9, 13, 18, 22, 25–27).

Israel will be blessed among the nations, and by God's providence, the Gentiles left on earth will be blessed through her. All of this illustrates again and confirms that the church in mystery was taken in the rapture seven years prior and has a heavenly citizenship. But, Israel finally receives her earthly kingdom promise from God. "Oh house of Judah, and house of Israel; so will I save you and ye shall be a blessing" (Zechariah 8:13). "Yea, many people and strong nations shall come to seek the LORD of hosts in Jerusalem, and to pray before the LORD." The people left on earth will take hold of the skirt of him that is a Jew, "saying, We will go with you for we have heard that God is with you" (Zechariah 8:22–23). This scene is set in the millennium, and it has no reference to the church.

"And it shall come to pass that everyone that is left of all nations which came against Jerusalem shall even go up from year to year to worship the King, the Lord of hosts, and to keep the Feast to Tabernacles" (Zechariah 14:16). This is in the millennium, and there will be consequences for not coming to Jerusalem to worship the Lord. "And it shall be, that whoso will not come up of all the families of the earth unto Jerusalem to worship the King, the LORD of Hosts, even upon them shall be no rain" (Zechariah 14:17). In regards to Israel, "For the nation and the kingdom that will not serve thee shall perish; yea, those nations shall be utterly wasted" (Isaiah 60:12–16). The church is completely absent in this. It makes one wonder how people could put the church into this when there is no mention anywhere about it.

Thus, Israel goes into the millennium as the head of nations. This also shows forthrightly that there will be Gentile people from other nations even at the end of the tribulation, and they will go into the millennium and then into eternity upon the earth. They are obviously not the church in heaven, neither are they national Israel (Deuteronomy 28:13). The millennium will be a time of joy, holiness, glory, comfort, and also justice (Isaiah 9:7). At the end of the thousand-year millennium, there shall be a revolt among the offspring of the people left on the earth; but they will meet with swift destruction (Revelation 20:7–9). Following the great white-throne judgment, God's promises are still the same toward Israel. "Thy people also shall be righteous: They shall inherit the land forever" (Isaiah 60:21). The destiny of Israel is quite different from the church, and the remaining Gentiles on earth will be blessed only through Israel.

After the day of vengeance the Lord will "appoint unto them that mourn in Zion, to give unto them beauty for ashes, the oil of joy for mourning, the garment of praise for the spirit of heaviness; that they might be called trees of righteousness, the planting of the LORD, that he might be glorified" (Isaiah 61:3).

> And strangers shall stand and feed your flocks, and the sons of the alien shall be your plowmen and your vinedressers. But ye shall be named the Priests of the LORD: men shall call you the Ministers of our God: and ye shall eat the riches of the Gentiles, and in their glory shall ye boast yourselves.
>
> Isaiah 61:5–6

"The whole earth is at rest, and is quiet: they break forth into singing" (Isaiah 14:7).

God has a wonderfully grand and royal plan for all people throughout all the ages. Then, when at the end of all things, it says, "And I saw a new heaven and a new earth: for the first heaven and the first earth were passed away; and there was no more sea." Now with finality the long ages have ended, it ends with the reckoning of time. "And I John saw the holy city, New Jerusalem, coming down from God out of heaven, prepared as a bride adorned for her husband" (Revelation 21:1–2). Even when there is a new heaven and a new earth, the Jews will still inherit the land forever. "That in the dispensation of the fullness of times he might gather together in one all things in Christ, both which are in heaven, and which are on earth; even in him" (Ephesians 1:10). This shows that there are two programs, one on earth and one in heaven, the Lord is working out all of this for his glory. "This same King they see, with the wounds in his hands, has healed up their wounds and here he stands."

The family of God from of old
They await the bride to behold
Now made perfect they proclaim
as our friends and family can attend
The Lamb's wedding in the end
Oh the marriage of the Lamb
and all creation will see
What the redeemed of the Son of God will finally be
Saints of old cry Alleluia
For the marriage of the Lamb has come
His wife hath made herself ready
As they all
Celebrate the royal wedding
In the heavenly banquet hall

The Old Testament Saints

Sometimes people within the church will get confused about the church's position in Christ and how it relates to the Old Testament saints. Many times people want to pronounce that the Old Testament saints are part of the church. They will say, why are we any better than the Old Testament saints? It really is an easy answer though unlooked for by many. We aren't better, but we do have a better covenant established upon better promises (Hebrews 8:6; 11:13, 39). Simply put, the Old Testament saints are our friends and relatives in heaven. They will attend the bride's wedding to Christ. Some people have a hard time understanding the different destinies of different people found throughout the Bible.

Here is an example that most people will understand right away. Israel as a nation will inherit the land forever, and there are plenty of Scriptures about that. Now obviously, Israel is not part of the church because Israel inherits the Land forever, upon the earth, and the church has a heavenly destiny in heaven (John 15:19; 17:16). As the church, we are strangers and pilgrims in this world. This simply points out that there are different peoples in the Bible with different destinies. If people can accept that as fact, then why is it so profound for some to see that there are other groups of people in the Bible?

Are we to imagine that the Gentile nations on earth during the millennium are somehow part of the church? Those people missed the rapture of the church, and they went through the tribulation and ended up on earth through the millennium. There is no way they can be the church, and there is no way they can be Israel; but they will go into eternity not being a part of Israel or the church. It is easy to recognize that group, but for some unexplained reason people struggle with thinking that the Old Testament saints are not part of the church. This isn't consistent though with the other groups of people that go into eternity as something other than the bride of Christ. The New Testament in his blood is not retroactive; it doesn't go back and include all the Old Testament saints.

Think about it with a clear sightedness. If the Old Testaments saints have what we, the church, have, then why did Jesus have to come? What does the Bible say about these saints of old? First of all Jesus came because the sacrifices of old could never fully take away sin (Hebrews 10:1–10). Jesus went on to say, "There is not a greater prophet than John the Baptist, but he that is least in the kingdom of God is greater than he" (Luke 7:28). The kingdom of God concerns the church, and that is why this is said about he who is least in the kingdom of God being greater than John. Jesus shows the superiority of the new covenant over the old.

The faithful Old Testament saints are not part of the church, or bride. Luke 16:16 says, "The law and the prophets were until John: since that time the Kingdom of God is preached, and every man presseth into it." For a testament to be valid, there must be a death of a testator. "A Testament is of force after men are dead: otherwise it is of no strength at all while the testator liveth" (Hebrews 9:15–17). This reveals that the New Testament in his blood did not become effective until Jesus was crucified and died. That is when the veil was rent, and now we can come boldly to the throne of grace. The saints of the Old Testament would include all those up to and including John the Baptist. The law and the prophets were until John. John the Baptist verifies this point even further in John 3:29: "He that hath the bride is the Bridegroom: but the friend of the bridegroom, which standeth and heareth him, rejoiceth greatly because of the Bridegroom's voice: this my joy therefore is fulfilled. He must increase, but I must decrease." There are at least four things that are shown here in (John 3:29–30).

1. John the Baptist identifies Jesus as the bridegroom. (He was standing there listening to the bridegroom's voice.)
2. John did not identify himself with the bride or the church.
3. John calls himself the friend of the bridegroom, and it helps to establish a difference. Thus, the Old Testament saints are

friends of the bridegroom, and that is their role in heaven at the marriage of the Lamb.

4. John said, "He must increase, but I must decrease." John recognized the change in Testaments.

The church has a better covenant, which was established upon better promises (Hebrews 8:6). In Hebrews chapter eleven, the saints of old were commended for their faith, but these all died in faith, not having received the promises. They saw them afar off, and were persuaded of them, and embraced them, and confessed that they were strangers and pilgrims on the earth (Hebrews 11:13). This is not to say that the saints of old won't be in heaven, for we know that they will. The Bible clearly teaches that they were seeking a heavenly country (Hebrews 11:13–16).

Addressing the saints of the Old Testament, it says,

> Of whom the world was not worthy: they wandered in deserts, and in mountains, and in dens and caves of the earth. And these all, having obtained a good report through faith, received not the promise: God having provided some better thing for us, that they without us should not be made perfect.
>
> Hebrews 11:38–40

It is repeated over and over in chapter eleven of Hebrews that they, the Old Testament saints, received not the promise. To throw light on it even further it says, God having provided some better thing for us, and this is a promise for the church. Furthermore on this same description it says that they without us should not be made perfect. The point is they are not us. We are the bride; they are friends of the Bridegroom (John 3:29). As blessed as they will be, they will not be the bride. So then we know that they will be in heaven, but they are not the church (Luke 7:28). They are our relatives in heaven who will attend our wedding and celebrate with us forever.

What else might the saints of old have then? Revelation 19:6–7 shows a great multitude shouting hallelujah!

> And I heard as it were the voice of a great multitude, and as the voice of many waters, and as the voice of mighty thunderings, saying, Alleluia: for the LORD God omnipotent reigneth. Let us be glad and rejoice, and give honour to him: for the marriage of the Lamb has come, and his wife hath made herself ready.
>
> Revelation 19:6-7

This shows a glorious picture of the Old Testament saints in heaven proclaiming the marriage of the Lamb. They are the friends of the bridegroom; they are there at our wedding. As John the Baptist proclaimed the coming of the Lamb of God, now the Old Testament saints herald the wedding of the Lamb in heaven! What a grand picture of a royal wedding in heaven, as it includes both groups of saints. They did not say, "We have made ourselves ready." In verse eight the bride is clothed in fine linen, bright and clean; for the fine linen is the righteous acts of the saints. This is the gleaming destiny of the church as the bride of Christ. The destiny of the Old Testament saints is to be with us as part of the family of God. They won't be the bride, but they are with us, under the roof of heaven as our relatives.

Blessed are those who are invited to the marriage supper of the Lamb. The bride is not invited; she is there because of her position. Think of it like this: is there a culture anywhere in the world that invites the bride to her own wedding? Of course not, but the friends of the bridegroom are invited. Looking back at Hebrews 11:40, where it says that they without us should not be made perfect, think of the joy they will have at the marriage of the Lamb. They will not be made perfect until the marriage supper comes. For without us (the bride), they should not be made perfect, for they cannot sit at the bridegroom's table until the marriage supper. They will also be a part of the armies of heaven that return with the Lord at the end of the tribulation.

Blessed are those who are invited to the marriage supper of the Lamb (Revelation 19:9). In John 3:29, John the Baptist says, "Because of the bridegroom's voice my joy therefore is fulfilled." Think of how much more he will be blessed when the marriage of the Lamb has come and his joy has been made perfect. We can't even imagine what the Lord has in store for us because it hasn't entered into our minds yet. Just imagine though, the family of God at the marriage supper of the Lamb, Old and New Testament saints together rejoicing. The church makes up all those who have died in Christ since the cross, and this goes only up to the rapture.

When the Lord comes for the body of Christ, it will be whole and without spot or wrinkle. The church will be presented as a chaste virgin to Jesus Christ (2 Corinthians 11:2). And this will be the whole body of Christ. All of this only underscores how the proceedings are to be in heaven: the Old and New Testament saints together in heaven at the royal wedding. Even though we can't imagine these things properly, we still get a glimpse of the awe and wonder of its pageantry. We will be surrounded by the holy angels, and we are told by an angel, "I am thy fellowservant, and of thy brethren that have the testimony of Jesus" (Revelation 19:10). This shows that one day we will have a proper and close relationship with the angels of God. All of this just hints at the grandeur and vastness of what the Lord has prepared for those who love him!

Some people have tried to say that because national Israel was the wife of God in the Old Testament then she has to be part of the bride of Christ. Remember that Israel played the whorish wife that was unfaithful in the Old Testament. The church has been espoused as a virgin bride to Christ. It is impossible to reconcile the English language by trying to say that a whore is the same as a virgin. So the wife of the Old Testament could never be the bride of Christ. The church will rejoice when she sees all of the relatives on the wedding day. The Old Testament saints have longed to see this day, and they will rejoice right along with us, as we're all then made perfect. "His wife hath made herself ready, as they all celebrate the royal wedding in the heavenly banquet hall."

The Gospel of John views the two
We see John the Baptist and John the beloved two
One disappears as the new unfolds
But in John the beloved
The mysteries are told
He's the sheep to first hear his voice
It's Jesus that's calling
His sheep know his voice

Gospel of John

We come at last to this gospel which stands alone in that it does not include the apocalyptic statements of Jesus, which are so prevalent in the synoptic gospels of Matthew, Mark, and Luke. This is also the gospel that reveals to all disciples of Jesus that we have a heavenly home with the Lord and that we will be in him, just as Jesus is in the Father. Jesus does not reveal that we are to try to help set up the kingdom of God on earth. Jesus reveals to all believers that he has gone to prepare a place for us in heaven: "In my Father's house are many mansions: if it were not so, I would have told you. I go to prepare a place for you" (John 14:2).

The Gospel of John presents seven divisions.

1. Opening preamble 1:1–14 showing who Jesus was in eternity and that this light came into the darkness.
2. The witness of John the Baptist as the voice crying in the wilderness making straight the way. The ending dispensation for John the Baptist and the prophets at the close of chapter three. John the Baptist also declares Jesus as the Lamb of God, and he bears record that Jesus is the Son of God (John 1:15–34).
3. The public ministry of Jesus is seen from John 1:35–12:50.
4. The private and intimate ministry to the disciples, concerning the Holy Spirit and heaven (John 13:1–17:26).
5. The sacrifice of Christ on the cross (John 18:1–19:42).
6. The Resurrection (John 20:1–31).
7. The epilogue showing Christ, the Lord and master. (John 21:1–25).

John writes this gospel in total anonymity, preferring to see Jesus first, just as he followed along behind Jesus, to linger and to lie upon his breast and know he is the disciple whom Jesus loved. John opens with showing Jesus as the Word, with God from the beginning. "All things were made by him; and without him was not any thing made that was made" (John 1:3). "In him was life; and the life was the light of men. And the light shineth in darkness; and the darkness comprehended it not" (John 1:4–5).

John himself is not mentioned or identified in the Gospel of John. He is always seen as though you were looking at an image, like the disciple whom Jesus loved, mysterious and a representation of something greater than himself. In the Gospel of John, he is but a shadow upon the pages of Scripture. This helps us discern that there is a great light shining upon John. The identity of John is seen in mystery because John signifies a type of the church or beloved, as the church is also seen in mystery all throughout the New Testament. "This is a great mystery: but I speak concerning Christ and the church" (Ephesians 5:32). What a glorious type we perceive when we see these great shadows and realize there is a heavenly light shining upon the life of John.

Jesus tells of entering in by the door into the sheepfold.

> Verily verily, I say unto you, He that entereth not by the door into the sheepfold, but climbeth up some other way, the same is a thief and a robber. But he that entereth in by the door is the shepherd of the sheep. To him the porter openeth; and the sheep hear his voice: and he calleth his own sheep by name, and leadeth them out.
>
> John 10:1–3

It is very interesting that John is the one who recognizes the voice of Jesus as Jesus stood on the shore and called to the disciples (John 21:6–7). For we know "the sheep follow him: for they know his voice" (John 10:4). It is John that is always seen as a type of the church (as the beloved), or in this case as a sheep. It is fitting that it is John who hears the voice of the good shepherd as he so beautifully typifies the church yet again (John 10:11, Revelation 4:1).

John the beloved was also not martyred. In typology this once again points to John as the espoused beloved. All the other apostles were martyred, another intriguing example that hints at the church.

> Then Peter, turning about, seeth the disciple whom Jesus loved following; which also leaned on his breast at supper, and said, Lord, which is he that betrayeth thee? Peter seeing him [John] saith to Jesus, Lord, and what shall this man do? Jesus saith unto him, If I will that he tarry till I come, what is that to thee? Follow thou me. Then went this saying abroad among the brethren, that that disciple should not die: yet Jesus said not unto him, He shall not die; but, If I will that he tarry till I come, what is that to thee?
>
> John 21:20–23

The Scriptures have this unusual reference here in the book of John as it relates to John (the disciple whom Jesus loved) not dying, but Jesus wasn't saying that John would not die. What was he referring to, and why did the brethren get so excited about this?

The only other explanation is again found in the typology of John, a picture of the church not dying. Jesus wasn't referring to John specifically, but this reference leaves the door open for the beloved not dying; and that is what the brethren thought about John. It was more a declaration for the church in the future; it's just that John signifies the church. It's very hard to describe this portion of Scripture in any other way other than in the light of John the beloved typifying the church in the future. Jesus allowed it because he wasn't referring to John not dying. No, it was about his church one day in the future. This was not a picture of confusion but rather a foreshadowing of the church presented to us about the beloved. What a magnificent picture this is! It's a scene of his church still on earth when he calls his bride and those not seeing death. This is what peaked the interest of the brethren, that a believer would not die but tarry until, in the words of Jesus, "till I come" (John 21:22–23).

Then John the beloved is given the Revelation of Jesus Christ later in the book of Revelation where he is caught up through the door into the sheepfold (Revelation 4:1). He is again seen as a type of the church being raptured out of this world and into the presence of the Lord and before his throne. The typology of John is a complete picture, and that is why evangelical Christians recognize John as a type of the church in Revelation 4:1. John, as a type of the church, proclaims who Jesus is from eternity (John 1:1–14). John is the one who consistently says that all who trust in the Son of God have eternal life (John 3:36; 20:31; 1 John 4:15; 5:5, 10–12, 20). It is John who first hears the voice of the Good Shepherd (John 21:7). It is John who is caught up through the sheepfold door into heaven (Revelation 4:1).

The Gospel of John is also intriguing in that it is paralleling the book of Revelation at times. There are many similarities in phrasing and precepts that go between the books. This was already mentioned in the chapter "The Church Age and the Rapture." Below are some examples of how certain thoughts and words run through both the Gospel of John and the book of Revelation. This list is only a partial list. Note, all of these thoughts and sayings are found in similar placement in each book. It was man that added the chapters and verses.

Gospel of John	Revelation
1:1 "In the beginning was the Word… and the Word was God."	1:1–2 John, "Who bare record of the Word of God, and the testimony of Jesus Christ"
1:5 "And the light shineth in the darkness; and the darkness comprehended it not."	1:14 "His head and his hairs were like wool, as white as snow; and his eyes were as a flame of fire."
1:14 "We beheld his glory, the glory as of the only begotten of the Father."	1:5–6 "Jesus Christ… the first begotten of the dead… to him be glory."
1:42 Jesus beheld Peter and said to him, "Thou shalt be called Cephas," a stone.	2:17 To him that overcometh…"will give him a white stone, and in the stone a new name written."

2:17 Jesus purges the temple: "The zeal of thine house hath eaten me up"	3:19 Jesus purifies his church: "be zealous therefore, and repent"
5:18 He had "broken the Sabbath" (the seventh day)	5:5 "the Lion of the tribe of Juda . . . hath prevailed to open the book, and to loose the seven seals"
5:27 The Father "hath given him authority to execute judgment."	5:7 "And he came and took the book out of the right hand of him that sat upon the throne."
5:25 "the dead shall hear the voice of the Son of God."	4:1–2 "a trumpet talking with me . . . Come up hither . . . behold, a throne was set in heaven."
5:43 "if another shall come in his own name, him ye will receive."	6:2 "behold a white horse and he . . . went forth conquering, and to conquer" (Antichrist)
6:35 "I am the bread of life: he that cometh to me shall never hunger . . . shall never thirst."	7:16 "They shall hunger no more, neither thirst any More."
7:38 "out of his belly shall flow rivers of living water."	7:17 "shall lead them unto living fountains of water."
11:25 "I am the resurrection, and the life: he that believeth in me, though he were dead, yet shall he live:"	11:12 "voice from heaven saying unto them, Come up hither. And they ascended up to heaven in a cloud."
12:25 "He that loveth his life shall lose it"	12:11 "They loved not their lives unto the death."
13:29 "because Judas had the bag" (controlled money)	13:17 "And that no man might buy or sell, save he that had the mark" (controls money)

14:15 "If ye love me, keep my commandments."

14:12 "Here is the patience of the saints: here are they that keep the commandments of God."

16:33 "I have overcome the world."

17:14 "And the Lamb shall overcome them."

17:12 "none of them is lost, but the son of Perdition"

17:8 "The beast… shall ascend… and go into perdition."

19:2 "And the soldiers platted a crown of thorns, and put it on his head"

19:12 "His eyes were as a flame of fire, and on his head were many crowns."

19:2 "they put on him a purple robe"

18:16 "that great city… was clothed in fine linen, and purple"

19:13 Pilate "sat down in the judgment seat in a place called the Pavement."

20:11–12 "And I saw a great white throne, and him that sat on it."

19:14 "and he saith unto the Jews, Behold your King!"

19:11 "And I saw heaven opened, and behold a white horse; and he that sat called Faithful and True."

19:19 "Pilate wrote a title… the writing was, JESUS OF NAZARETH THE KING OF THE JEWS."

19:16 "he hath on his vesture and on his thigh a name written, KING OF KINGS, AND LORD OF LORDS."

19:23 "when they had crucified Jesus, they took his garments"

19:13 "And he was clothed with a vesture dipped in blood"

20:27 "Be not faithless but believing"

21:8 "But the fearful, and unbelieving"

20:15 "Jesus saith unto her, Woman, why weepest thou?"

21:4 "And God shall wipe away all tears from Their eyes;"

20:30–31 "many other signs truly did Jesus in the presence of his disciples, which are not written in this book: But these are written, that ye might believe that Jesus is the Christ, the Son of God; and that believing ye might have life through his name."	20:15 "And whoever was not found written in the book of life was cast into the lake of fire."
21:12 "Jesus saith unto them, Come and Dine."	21:3 "and he will dwell with them, and they shall be his people, and God himself shall be with them."

The Mysterious Disappearance

There is another parallel that is truly fascinating, especially in the harvest sunset of golden light that shines out from all these previous examples. It's the placement of John 3:29 with John the Baptist and the saints of old, with the connection to the closing statements of Jesus to the seven churches in Revelation 3:22, and then John is caught up to heaven (Revelation 4:1). John the Baptist defines who he is along with the rest of the Old Testament saints when he says, "He that hath the bride is the bridegroom: but the friend of the bridegroom, which standeth and heareth him, rejoiceth greatly because of the bridegroom's voice: this my joy therefore is fulfilled. He must increase, but I must decrease". John the Baptist recognizes that he is not part of the bride and that there is a change in covenants about to take place. He had just declared of Jesus, "Behold the Lamb of God!" (John 1:36). But John the Baptist still speaks as a saint representing the last of the Old Testament saints and how they would all diminish. So the Old Testament saints come to the end of the age, of the law, and John the Baptist recognized their time being over, with the coming of the Messiah. He then vanishes from sight in the Gospel of John and is no longer seen in the Gospel of John!

It is amazing to realize that if the Gospel of John is paralleling with the book of Revelation, then this disappearance of the church in Revelation 4:1 now parallels with the Old Testament saints and how they disappeared from view in the same place in the Gospel of John! Both groups disappear (conveniently) in the same place in the Gospel of John and in the book of Revelation!

This has dramatic significance, with what has been shown already; both books are paralleling, and now we see this mysterious disappearance of the saints of old and the church. Here is the mystery of the resurrection: both groups that make up the family of God, the church as the bride of Christ and the Old Testament saints as friends of the bridegroom, disappear! They are no longer mentioned (on earth) due to the first resurrection taking place, as seen in Revelation 4:1, and now, they are both in heaven together as the family of God, and this is why we see the twenty-four elders before the throne (Revelation 4:4). For "they without us should not be made perfect" (Hebrews 11:40). "Wherefore seeing we are compassed about with so great a cloud of witnesses" (Hebrews 12:1). It's such a great cloud of witnesses because it includes all the church-age saints and also the Old Testament saints together as the family of God.

It is a fact that the Gospel of John is paralleling with the book of Revelation at times, and it is a fact that both groups disappear from view at the same place in each book thereby giving substantial evidence for the rapture as seen in Revelation 4:1. John the Baptist representing the Old Testament saints, and John the beloved representing the saints within in the church age. The timing of their disappearances shines a dazzling bright light on the pre-trib rapture of the church. I don't see how people who are mid-trib or post-trib can argue against this beautiful imagery of good things to come presented to us from both the Gospel of John and the book of Revelation. Both groups of saints vanish away and are no longer seen. It is exciting to see these precepts laid out in front of us, paralleled, "For precept must be upon precept, precept upon precept; line upon line, line upon line; here a little, and there a little" (Isaiah 28:10).

As the church, we sometimes forget that the Old Testament saints will be resurrected in the first resurrection right along with all believers that came in the church age. They wouldn't be excluded from being resurrected at this same time. Even the martyrs of Revelation are a part of the first resurrection, although they follow seven years later at the end of the tribulation as being the gleanings of the harvest as it's seen within the seven days of the Feast of Tabernacles.

The Apostle John proclaims for all believers in the church age what is required for salvation. "He that believeth on the Son hath everlasting life: and he that believeth not the Son shall not see life; but the wrath of God abideth on him" (John 3:36). We see the Old Testament saints in John 3:29. Then we see the qualifying requirements for all believers within the church age. Then the church is gone in Revelation 4:1. Just as the Old Testament prophets vanished from sight, as John the Baptist said, "I must decrease." It's all pointing to that great event and disappearance in the rapture, the first resurrection that includes both Old and New Testament saints.

Major Themes of the Bible Seen in John Chapter Five

As touched on already, the Gospel of John is at times paralleling with the book of Revelation. Chapter five of John has some of the most major themes and declarations in it.

With the first major theme we see that "the Father judgeth no man, but hath committed all judgment unto the Son" (John 5:22). As already pointed out, this has to do with the parallels found in chapters four through five of Revelation. The Lamb standing up is a major dispensational change, because (Jesus the Lamb) is no longer sitting upon the throne of grace (Hebrews 4:16, Colossians 3:1). The time of the church age has ended, and judgment is about to begin with the opening of the seals. This is when the Lord is also seen arising to shake the earth (Isaiah 2:19–21; 3:13). The Lamb rises; the scene in heaven is about to quicken (Revelation 5:6, Job 19:25, Psalm 94:1–2, Zechariah 14:4).

Then the first resurrection is seen in John 5:25. "Verily, verily, I say unto you, The hour is coming, and now is, when the dead shall hear the voice of the Son of God: and they that hear shall live." The church will hear the voice of the Son of God; this is the first resurrection. This is seen when John the beloved is caught up in Revelation 4:1. Then we see the twenty-four elders are before the throne having received their crowns. Blessed is he who has part in the first resurrection.

Interestingly enough after the resurrection is spoken of in John 5:25, then judgment starts. This is a clear indication of the rapture happening first and then the judgment that follows.

John 5:27 then goes right back to the idea of judgment, and you'll notice it follows after Jesus just commented about the first resurrection. "And hath given him authority to execute judgment also, because he is the Son of man." After the resurrection as seen in Revelation 4:1, the Lamb stands, ending the time of grace. Now, the Lamb goes and takes the book out of the right hand of him who sits upon the throne. There is only one reason that this happens, and it concerns judgment, or the vengeance of our God (Isaiah 61:1–2). Jesus the Lamb now receives the authority to judge the earth. The next thing following the Lamb receiving authority is the seals, as they are opened in Revelation 6:2. Notice how judgment is talked about after the first resurrection is mentioned. As we have seen, the Gospel of John is paralleling with the book of Revelation at times; it is the order that is so astounding! The first resurrection has the reward of crowns; then the Lamb stands, ending the time of grace. Then comes the judgment, as it starts with the Jews accepting the antichrist as predicted in John 5:43 and fulfilled in Revelation 6:2.

Even the second resurrection is mentioned in John 5:28–29. "Marvel not at this: for the hour is coming in which all that are in the graves shall hear his voice, And shall come forth; they that have done good, unto the resurrection of life; and they that have done evil, unto the resurrection of damnation." The term Son of God is not used here because that is a distinct term used for believers and the believers were already caught up to heaven in the first resurrection as mentioned in verse twenty-five. This is the second resurrection spoken of here, and it happens at the great white throne after the millennium.

John 5:43 shows that the Jews will not accept Jesus, but they will accept another in his own name. Revelation 6:2 starts the tribulation with the rider on the white horse, thus the Jews have been deceived as Jesus predicted. The first resurrection has already taken place as shown earlier in John 5:25 and paralleled in Revelation 4:1. I love the fact that Jesus talks of the first resurrection before he talks about judgment, and then we see the coming deception that awaits the Jews in John 5:43. Jesus himself sets the timing here, the resurrection first, then the deception of the Jews by the antichrist (John 5:43, Revelation 6:2).

All of John 5 from verse nineteen to the end of the chapter is Jesus responding to the Jews and their rejection of him and the consequences of their rejection. This is why all these things are mentioned in the order they are, as they tie directly into Daniel's seventieth week as seen in the book of Revelation, especially as the Lamb starts judgment with the opening of the seals in Revelation 6. The first resurrection has already taken place, and the twenty-four elders are before the throne. Second resurrection comes later, but now everything focuses on the Jews in the seven-year tribulation. This is how John 5 reads, and it is mirrored in Revelation 4–5 and 6:2.

The deity of Christ is focused on in the Gospel of John. John shows Jesus as the eternal Word that came from eternity who took on the form of a man. "And the Word was made flesh, and dwelt among us, (and we beheld his glory as of the only begotten of the Father,) full of grace and truth" (John 1:14). We see that by receiving him, we receive power. "But as many as received him, to them gave he the power to become the sons of God, even to them that believe on his name" (John 1:12). Even John the Baptist, the last of the Old Testament prophets, declares that Jesus is the Son of God when he says, "And I saw, and bare record that this is the Son of God" (John 1:34). Jesus proclaims his deity when he says. "I am the bread of life" (John 6:35). "I am the light of the world" (John 8:12; 9:5). "I am the door" (John 10:7, 9). "I am the good shepherd" (John 10:11, 14). "I am the resurrection and the life" (John 11:25).

"I am the way, the truth, and the life" (John 14:6). "I am the true Vine" (John 15:1).

Then the all-encompassing statement by Jesus. "Then said the Jews unto him, Thou art not yet fifty years old, and hast thou seen Abraham? Jesus said unto them, Verily, verily, I say unto you, Before Abraham was, I am" (John 8:57–58). This statement confirms the deity of Jesus as the Jews then took up stones to cast at him (John 8:59). "But Jesus hid himself, and went out of the temple, going through the midst of them, and so passed by."

Jesus Heals on the Sabbath

"And as Jesus passed by, he saw a man which was blind from his birth" (John 9:1). This shows the love of Christ for those in need, even as he had just come out of the midst of them who wanted to stone him. He still had the time to stop and minister and heal the man who was blind from his birth. The "disciples asked him, saying, Master, who did sin, this man, or his parents, that he was born blind? Jesus answered, Neither hath this man sinned, nor his parents: but that the works of God should be manifest in him" (John 9:2–3).

This story is humorous in that the blind man just gives an honest answer when questioned by the Jews. They asked him, "What did he to thee? How opened he thine eyes?" (John 9:26). "He answered them, I have told you already, and ye did not hear: wherefore would ye hear it again? Will ye also be his disciples?" This really stirred up their anger: "Then they reviled him." Then, in an almost dead-pan and humorous response, he says, "Why herein is a marvelous thing, that ye know not from whence he is, and yet he hath opened mine eyes" (John 9:30). There is a sense of humor built into this account in the Scripture with the majesty of who Jesus is as the Son of God shining bright. Then the former blind man declares to the Jews, who already know. He says, "Since the world began was it not heard that any man opened the eyes of one that was born blind. If this man were not of God, he could do nothing" (John 9:33–34). The Jews being angered cast him out of the temple. Jesus hears of this and seeks the man out and asks him, "Dost thou believe on the Son of God?" (John 9:35).

This is a splendid and very accurate picture of how we are all blind, until we believe on Jesus, the Son of God. This also confirms our previous chapters in that the church believes on, and will hear the voice of the Son of God, not the Son of man because the Son of man concerns the Jews.

Intimate Moments with His Disciples

In chapter thirteen, Jesus gathers the disciples together for the Passover supper, and in his abounding love for the disciples, he washes their feet. Peter protests that Jesus would never wash his feet until Jesus says, "If I wash thee not, thou hast no part of with me. Simon Peter saith unto him, Lord, not my feet only, but also my hands and my head" (John 13:2–9). Jesus then goes on to reveal who would betray him, and then in verse thirty-three he calls the disciples little children. And in verse thirty-four Jesus says, "A new commandment I give unto you, That ye love one another; as I have loved you, that ye also love one another." The emphasis of love is placed here by Jesus to show what he expects from his disciples thereafter.

In chapter fourteen Jesus tells them, "Let not your heart be troubled: ye believe in God, believe also in me. In my Father's house are many mansions: if it were not so, I would have told you. I go to prepare a place for you. And if I go and prepare a place for you, I will come again, and receive you unto myself; that where I am, there ye may be also" (John 14:1–3). Much of the confusion with replacement theology and the emerging church of today would be corrected right here if people would read this and understand that we are not of this world. We will not inherit the land on earth like the Jews because right here in Scripture it's telling us we will dwell in mansions in heaven and that Jesus will come for us personally. The emerging church here misses the whole point of us belonging in heaven. We should not be trying to bring about peace so we can all have a fancy house here on earth. This is not what Jesus was revealing to his church.

Jesus then sends the comforter, "And I will pray the Father, and he shall give you another Comforter, that he may abide with you for ever" (John 14:16). As Christians, we have the Holy Spirit, who shall guide us into all truth, and one of the most remarkable statements made is when Jesus says in John 15:19 that we are not of this world. "If ye were of the world, the world would love his own: but because ye are not of the world, but I have chosen you out of the world, therefore the world hateth you." Anyone that embraces replacement theology or that is involved in the emerging church will have to completely disregard these Scriptures. We have not replaced Israel, and we are not to set up a business model to enrich ourselves because we are not part of this world. These are the days of ignorance when people feel they can disregard the Scriptures that speak clearly about these things.

In contrast to what emerging church leaders might say, Jesus says this about his true disciples: "They are not of the world, even as I am not of the world" (John 17:16). Jesus goes on in John 17:21–24 to pray that his followers will share in the glory with Jesus and the Father in heaven. We are to preach the gospel of our Lord and Savior to this dying world, sharing with all who will listen the message of forgiveness through Jesus sacrifice on the cross. We need to continue along the narrow way with an expectancy of his return at any moment. "But the end of all things is at hand: be ye therefore sober, and watch unto prayer" (1 Peter 4:7). "And when the chief Shepherd shall appear, ye shall receive a crown of glory that fadeth not away" (1 Peter 5:4).

Conclusion

We have looked at the many types and precepts in the Bible that only demonstrate his gracious designs for a pre-trib rapture for his church. One will wait a long time until they see someone try to discount or explain away all of these foreshadowing types. They may talk against them, but it is a much harder thing using Scripture to write about them to gloss over all of them using the Bible. Even people who hold different views on the rapture recognize this. It's a dangerous thing going out your door to set out to twist and deny all of these precepts that are so clothed in light from above. The types presented here shine brightly on the pre-trib view, which are precepts of the blessed hope. Like the great shadows seen under clouds, they reveal to us that truly there is a great light shining on all these things. If people refuse to look at these precepts that are clearly seen from the Scriptures, they will end up with an inaccurate view of prophecy. If they are Christian, we hope that they would be open to exploring Scripture to see with their waking eyes what the truth would call forth.

Nowadays people with biased and personal prejudices feel they need to discredit the KJV of the Bible. They do this to put the church into the tribulation; but it is not an honest thing to do, and it is downright deceptive to pretend that the twenty-four elders are now all of a sudden angels or other beings. Nor is it scriptural to say that the church has taken the place of Israel when the Lord says he will not give those promises to another. It is also a silly thing for churches to seek to bring all peoples together to help bring about the kingdom of God on earth when we as the church are not of this world. This kind of thinking only leads to error and disbelief in the Bible. The Bible tells us what will happen in the end, and it is unfortunate that some Christians think they are going to bring about peace on earth when the entire book of Revelation tells us of the apocalypse and what will happen in the end.

We need to study God's Word using a good translation or preferably the (received text) KJV, without which this book would not make sense, and without which this book could not have been written. It also affirms that there is a problem in other translations. We need to share the gospel with all who will listen, sharing the whole truth. It is my prayer that people will look at this book with all the precepts that are illustrated and then realize in their hearts that we need to be looking for the blessed hope, that we might hear the voice of the Great Shepherd, that we would see the precepts of the blessed hope and know that a great light has revealed them. All praise be to Jesus, our Lord and Savior.

About the Author

Don Mills was born in Princeton, British Columbia, Canada in 1953. He accepted the Lord in 1974, and after studying the Bible for a few years Don started writing about the Bible. About 1990 Don noticed that some of his friends were all of a sudden starting to question some basic Bible beliefs. He felt the need to write about those things, but as the writings progressed over the years, it became apparent that these writings were more for the whole body of Christ. Don married Lois Lindley from Arcata, California, in 1977, they have 3 children, Rachel, Travis, and Justen. Don worked for Arcata Redwood for 19 years while raising his family, he then moved to Twin Falls, Idaho. Don & Lois then went to work for the CSN radio ministry in it's infancy. They watched as CSN grew into a national radio network. Don has been the Station manager of KAWZ, the up link station for CSN since it's beginning in 1995. Don is also the Program Director for the Christian Satellite Network.

References

Bible references are primarily from the King James, Scofield Study Bible. Oxford University Press, 1996.

Buksbazen, Victor. The Gospel in the Feasts of Israel. The Friends of Israel Gospel Ministry, 1954. Chapter 5.

Chafer, Lewis Sperry. Systematic Theology. Vol. 4. Dallas: Dallas Seminary Press, 1948. 47.

Charles, R.H. The Book of Jubilees, Chapter 16, Orig. Pub. 1917, Revisions 2003 by the Book Tree. Abraham Celebrates Feast.

Deems, Charles F. The Light of the Nations. 1884. Part VI, Chapter 1 from, "At the Feast of Tabernacles," 448. Seventy bulls sacrificed for the nations.

Feast of Tabernacles. <www.Biblestudent.com>.

Feinberg, Charles Lee. God Remembers: A Study of the Book of Zechariah. 1965. 261.

Gaster, Theodore. Festivals of the Jewish Year. New York: William Morrow, 1953. 98.

Geneva Bible. 1560. Hendrickson Publishers, 2007.

Glaser, Mitch and Zhava. The Fall Feasts of Israel. Moody Press, 1987. Chapters 13–16.

Gospel of John paralleling the book of Revelation. From PhD dissertation submitted to the University of Dallas, 2001.

Greek references mainly from <net.bible.org>.

Habershon, Ada R. Study of the Types. Kregal Publishing, 1993.

Henry, Matthew. Matthew Henry's Commentary, 1706, Comments on the twenty-four elders from Revelation chapters four and five.

Larkin, Clarence. Dispensational Truth. 1918. Clarence Larkin EST. "Types in the Bible." 153–155.

Lockyer. All the Parables of the Bible. Zondervan: 1963. Matthew 25. "Comments about the Ten Virgins." 237–240.

Nelson, Oliver. Dictionary Bible Literacy Thomas Nelson, 1989.

New American Standard Bible. Study edition. A.J. Holman Company, 1975.

NIV, Life Application Study Bible. Zondervan. Notes on Revelation 4 on the twenty-four elders.

Rogers, Adrian. Unveiling the End Times in Our Time. Broadman and Holman, 2004. "The Twenty-four Elders." 69.

Smith, Sir William. Smith's Bible Dictionary. Nashville: Thomas Nelson, 1813–1893. "Tabernacles." Later Edition.

Tabernacles, Feasts of Booths, Succot. <http://www.goodnewsmedia.com/bible.studies.htm>.

Taylor, Edward. Upon the Types of the Old Testament. Vol. 1. University of Nebraska Press, 1989. 3–4.

Throne Room and Seals Courtesy of the Digital Image Archive, Pitts Theology Library, Chandler School of Theology, Emory University.

Tyndale Bible. 1526. The British Library, in association with The Tyndale Society, Text Copyright 2000, Tyndale Society.

Way of Life Encyclopedia of the Bible and Christianity. Cloud, David W. 4th ed. 2002. Tabernacle and Bible Translations. 63–85, 567.

Welch, Charles. Dispensational Truth. 3rd ed. London: The Berean Publishing Trust, 1959. "The Mystery of Christ and the Earthly Kingdom." 45–47.

Wilson Old Testament Word Studies. Hendrickson Publishers. Fetch, Lamps.

Wycliffe Bible LV. BibleGateway.com, 2008. Gospel Communications International.

Wycliffe Commentary, 1962 version, on Matthew chapter 25.

Endnotes

1 Edward Taylor, 1693, Upon the Types of the Old Testament, Vol. 1, page 3, Unversity Nebraska Press 1989

2 Edward Taylor, 1693, Upon the Types of the Old Testament, Vol. 1, page 4. Unversity Nebraska Press 1989

3 Clarence Larkin, Dispensational Truth, page 155.

4 Clarence Larkin Dispensational Truth, page 154.

5 Clarence Larkin, Dispensational Truth, page 154.

6 Clarence Larkin, Dispensational Truth, page 154.

7 Clarence Larkin, Dispensational Truth, page 154.

8 http://goodnewsmedia.com/bible.com/bible.studies.htm/sg14.htm.

9 NIV Life Application Study Bible, Zondervan 1991, Revelation Ch 4 footnote.

10 Wilson's Old Testament Word Studies, Lees, page 248. Hendrickson Publishers.

11 The New Bible Dictionary, Lees, page 728. WM. B. Eerdmans Publishing Co.

12 http://websters-online-dictionary.org/definition/lees

13 Lewis Sperry Chafer, Systematic Theology, Vol. 4, page 4. Dallas Seminary Press, 1948

14 Lewis Sperry Chafer, Systematic Theology, Vol. 4, page 47. Dallas Seminary Press, 1948

listen|imagine|view|experience

AUDIO BOOK DOWNLOAD INCLUDED WITH THIS BOOK!

In your hands you hold a complete digital entertainment package. Besides purchasing the paper version of this book, this book includes a free download of the audio version of this book. Simply use the code listed below when visiting our website. Once downloaded to your computer, you can listen to the book through your computer's speakers, burn it to an audio CD or save the file to your portable music device (such as Apple's popular iPod) and listen on the go!

How to get your free audio book digital download:

1. Visit www.tatepublishing.com and click on the e|LIVE logo on the home page.
2. Enter the following coupon code: dea5-7707-5e72-8958-6262-8d2c-7ddf-aebd
3. Download the audio book from your e|LIVE digital locker and begin enjoying your new digital entertainment package today!

Made in the USA
San Bernardino, CA
15 August 2015